ENTREPR
STORI

CLARE MARTIN

CONTENTS

ABOUT THE BOOK

Entrepreneur Stories is a collection of real life Entrepreneur stories to inspire business owners to launch and scale their businesses.

Based upon the podcast Bloom By Blue Cactus, it humanises sustainable startup owners, telling the stories of how they started their businesses and how they've grown them. They open up about how they've financed their brands, the most important learnings and offer actionable top tips for other entrepreneurs.

Entrepreneur Stories is designed to demonstrate that entrepreneurs are REAL people. They aren't simply executives sitting behind a corporate desk. They are like you and me, some have families, some don't. Some work 24/7, others are able to take a step back when they want to.

Each of the business owners has a unique and engaging story to tell about their vision and their growth.

But one thing that brings them together is their drive to succeed in a cut throat world, where consumers are spoilt for choice and social media is vying for everyone's attention.

About The Author

Clare Martin is a sustainable marketer, helping ethical startups tell their stories to the people that matter. She's passionate about supporting small businesses to attract more clients through sharing their experience and their mission. She believes that being transparent with customers is the way to get them on your side and having great products is only a small part of the puzzle to gain traction in whatever market you're in.

Clare's background is in journalism and storytelling. She's a trained journalist with a degree in multimedia journalism and has worked as a features editor, editorial director and managing director at a brand content agency, where her primary role was strategising with both big businesses and startups to carry their message to the world.

She set up her first digital marketing agency in 2017 after the birth of her son, and transformed the focus in 2020 to follow her passions around sustainable startups.

She's worked with large corporations including Oracle, Microsoft, Inmarsat, although her interests now lie with smaller businesses making a big impact with their ideas, whether product or service-led brands.

In 2021, mid-pandemic, she set up her own eco lingerie business, Confident Tiger, which uses the skills she's built up over the last ten years to demonstrate a strong marketing strategy can go a long way to build global brands.

In this book, Clare shares her conversations with sustainable business owners that have invested in their ideas to create rapidly growing, successful businesses

INTRODUCTION

Entrepreneur Stories is a book to inspire any budding entrepreneurs, or small enterprise owners that want their business to grow fast.

Based on the hugely popular podcast series, 'Bloom by Blue Cactus', this book puts faces behind the stories and offers extra insight into these entrepreneurs' lives.

Entrepreneur Stories is a compilation of biographical learnings from some of the UK's biggest sustainable and dynamic startups, exploring their journey through business ownership. It introduces their business, their successes and failures. You'll be able to find out why they set up their company and how they've switched their focus when they've needed to.

It explores their ethical and sustainable values and their journey, including what kind of investment they've received and how they were able to grow their business from spending on the right things, at the right time.

These businesses have funded their vision through a range of different channels - it might be bootstrapping, reward-based or equity-based investment, or it could be through grants. Each story offers valuable insights into the world of running a sustainable business, from identifying the best way of finding investors, how to certify as a B Corp and get investment from people aligned with your values. It will help you identify where you should be spending your money and where you should hold back, how to outsource effectively, all from the people who have done it.

One thing these people all have in common is ambition and knowledge that their businesses will grow, however they opted to invest in their business.

Knowing what to invest in, and how to get investment is a vital first step when you are starting a business. Couple that with outsourcing to the most talented people in the industry, and you have a recipe for business success.

Follow these stories, and feel totally inspired about how your business can make a huge difference in the world.

Chapter One:
Jen Fuller - Etta Loves

WEBSITE: ettaloves.com

Etta Loves is a baby accessories brand with its roots in science and development. All of the company's products have been designed following extensive research into how a baby's eyes develop in their first year and turning that into baby essentials, such as muslins, playmats and sensory strips to encourage the development of their vision. It was all triggered by an outfit that founder Jen Fuller was wearing while on maternity leave.

When I had my first daughter, I already had a career that I was thoroughly enjoying and expecting to go back into, so I wasn't looking for a new business opportunity to arise, like some do when they're on maternity leave.

I remember it was a really cold February morning and I was sat feeding Etta. She had always been a fussy feeder, but all of a sudden I realised she was feeding really well. And I looked at her little face and she was staring at my black and white jumper, absolutely mesmerised by the patterns. I'd read somewhere that babies prefer black and whites, not only because of the high contrast, but the neurons in a baby's brain react to them differently, helping them focus and calming them in the process.

I thought it was really interesting and a magical thing to see. I glanced over to the very plain muslin on my shoulder, and I just had this flash of inspiration. I thought that if my patterned jumper was working for my daughter today, why couldn't I make a difference to other families' feeding experiences?

I wandered off to a baby sensory class that afternoon, chatted to my NCT friends and asked them whether they thought muslins could do a bit more, developmentally, than they currently do, using shapes and patterns and colours to make the child and parent have a better experience.

The first and most important thing I did was research to see if anything like it already existed like it.

Financially, we were fortunate enough that Etta was our first child, so it was my first maternity leave and maternity pay for my company was enough to pay for living. I'd been in a fairly well-paid job, so I'd actually managed to have some savings.

The starting point was something that's fairly small as a unit cost, and that was quite intentional. I didn't want to jump in and produce an entire range of multiple products. I thought muslins are something I could test the concept with and it wasn't going to cost me a fortune.

I've always been someone that's had loads of ideas, but none of them have ever really grabbed me enough to do anything about them. I ended up returning back to work in the October, the exact same week that the first wave of stock turned up and Etta Loves went live. So quite the challenge!

I've put so much effort particularly into Instagram, which is a bit of a double-edged sword. Some weeks I love it and some weeks I hate it, but it's undeniably a really good platform for spreading the word and finding people who are going to like what you do.

We're also fortunate because our designs are so bold and quite recognisable, so I think word of mouth has been really huge for us.

We've put so much effort into the design phase and we work with an orthoptist who puts scientific precision into them. This means they work, and when something works, people want to talk and rave about it.

Our growth has happened quite organically over the last few years, with the combination of babies being born, and the pandemic causing even more stress for new parents. There are usually classes like baby sensory that parents would take their babies to, but they've all had to be shut. Parents have been looking for ways to stimulate their baby at home, so the word has been slowly spreading.

From a direct marketing point of view, we've invested more in PPC and Facebook Ads. So I think we offered something at a time when people really needed it.

One of the very first things I did as soon as I could was move the fulfilment, so the physical packing and sending of orders moved into a warehouse. I've always believed that there were certain things that the Founder or the CEO doesn't need to do and picking and packing is one of those things. You do need to keep a handle on things and make sure every decision is really core to the brand, but things like posting out orders is not really necessary.

And I think as we've grown in these last nine months or so, there's been other things that I've realised I've needed to let go of to be able to focus on harnessing the growth. Growth is something that can unsteady you a little bit, because as a product business, we have a finite amount of stock and it's quite a long lead time on our stock, so I needed to be hot on our forecast, and our production timelines.

So I've invested in people, including an assistant who is amazing. All the customer service is now outsourced, because obviously with growth comes an increase in returns and questions about postage, adding gift notes and changing addresses. And that's one of those things that takes up a tremendous amount of my day and it doesn't need to be me doing it as long as it's someone with the right tone coming from Etta Loves.

And then I've also had to find more money to invest in stock, to keep up with the demand. I've invested in a merchandiser, so again, another person who was really starting to look at our numbers to see the growth, and the slower areas. This makes me think a little bit more strategically around what sells, what doesn't, and how do I best market the things I need to. So it's definitely been a combination of people.

I remember reading that founders should try and spend at least 30% of their week just doing nothing and thinking about business development.

I think it's so easy when you are a founder of a small business to juggle all of the business plates from accounting to stock management, to marketing, that you lose sight of the business as a whole. You're learning every single day and that's part of the joy, but it's also a lot of the pressure.

I've always been a big advocate in letting go of the things that you really don't need to do. In one way, it's gut-wrenching because I'm a bit of a control freak, and when it comes to something that you've nurtured and put actual blood, sweat, tears, and cash into, it feels risky. But I think as long as you find the right people and you hand over in the right way, so you sculpt how you want them to talk and behave and what to say and what not to say, and the overall kind of ethos of the brand, I think it's only ever a positive thing.

CHAPTER TWO:

JAYNE CLARK-DENYER - ORGANICALLY EPIC

WEBSITE: organicallyepic.uk

Organically Epic started in 2015 as a distribution business and has now flourished to become a manufacturer of organic dental care, including toothbrushes, tongue cleaners, cotton buds and vegan floss. Founder Jayne Clark-Denyer talks through how she made the transition from distributor to manufacturer in a few months and the challenges that come with producing your own goods.

We were originally buying from organic beauty companies that weren't available in the UK readily - mainly skincare, body care and tanning. We imported them to the UK and our remit was to get them into as many stores as possible. For a time, that worked really, really well, but what we worked out fairly quickly on is that we weren't really in control of what we did. We were our own business, but we were still beholden to these other brands and what they wanted and what we could do and what we could talk about. Also, money was coming in and money was going out so fast. We had a business and it was working, but we couldn't get to the next level and scale.

So towards the back end of 2018, I launched our first dental product, after I started becoming quite obsessed with dental and natural organic dental items. I couldn't find anything that I liked on the market. So we launched our charcoal-infused bamboo toothbrush in 2018 and it did really well.

Shortly after, we launched the next product and the next one and the next one. And within the year, we dropped all the other brands and we were no longer distributing for anyone else. We became our own fully-fledged, natural dental brand. It was a risk that was worth taking at the time, and it's a risk that's paid off. Even though there's less money coming in because the other products were bigger and more expensive, we're now making more money on what we're buying and we can scale a bit more and invest in ourselves.

Cashflow for any small business is key. I think when I first started out, I didn't really quite understand that so much. All of our money went into buying the products from brands and then distributing them, and money was tight. Before we launched our own product, we had to scale back what we were buying, in order to be able to have the money to then invest in our own products. I haven't had massive amounts of investment, but focused on bootstrapping rather than getting any outside investment.

And that's why we had to switch to manufacturing our own products quickly. It was a big risk and took me a year to decide that we were going to go full-force with our own products and find a manufacturer that I was happy with.

What it means though is I can make the decisions that I want to make and I can be the one to answer for those decisions instead of it being up in the air and being someone else telling me what to do.

I know quite a lot of skincare brands that have had venture capitalist investment and that's allowed them to scale very, very quickly and piggyback off their investors' knowledge.

And sometimes I feel that I should be doing that, but I just don't feel that it's right for me to scale that quickly and to also have these people to answer to, and obviously give money back to.

Previously, 90% of our income was through selling to stores and we've still got that, supplying to 50 or 60 currently. But that took a knock when Covid hit and we've had to really diversify and focus on 'direct to consumer' sales through our website and social channels. It was something that I should've done a long time ago, with a lot of our customers and peers telling me in the background they wanted to see a wider range of products on our website. Because we were happily growing on the stockist side, upping direct sales wasn't really on my radar, but that's something that I'm very much focused on now. I would really like more of an even split, with 50% going through the website and 50% with stockists.

Distribution is a big channel for us and the sales team is vital. They're speaking to potential stockists every day. We also invest quite a lot of money in doing the natural organic trade shows as well throughout the year, so we can speak to all the buyers for the major stores. One way to scale fast is to focus on wholesale, because it gets the bigger orders that allow the cashflow to happen faster, so you can invest in more Research & Development (R&D) and stock.

Another element I've invested in is personal development. I started studying with Formula Botanica just before my second daughter was born. It's taught me how to make skincare and really helped me on my dental journey as well, because I've been able to look at what can go into ingredient-based dental products. I've invested a lot of money in this, and doing it properly with the best people there are. And that's going to push the business forward in a way that I wouldn't have been able to do if I was just sitting at home tinkering on my own.

But what's important to remember when it comes to investment, is that every business is different, and every person that runs that business is different. There isn't any one way that you should be doing things and something that works for one person, even if they've got exactly the same business, doing exactly the same thing, may not work for the next. So how you market to them will be different, the type of products, ultimately the packaging or whatever would be different.

The key to successful business ownership is working out what you're interested in and what you want to do, but also the things that you don't want to do. Get somebody else to do the bits you're not skilled in or you don't enjoy doing, whether that's outsourcing, or if that's being able to hire somebody internally to do it for you.

If I could have done things differently, I would have listened to people around me, specifically, my brother actually, who, when we started distributing Australian dental brands that had similar-ish products to us, asked why I was doing it for somebody else and that I could do it myself. And told him I couldn't. I wish I'd have launched our own brand earlier, but then I wouldn't know what I know now. And maybe that would have been too soon, who knows?

I'd have also been more strategic about things. If you can't do it or you don't want to do it, find someone who can do it better. Of course, if it's your passion, then develop to be able to do it yourself.

And if it doesn't feel right, don't do it.

CHAPTER THREE

CLAUDIA GWINUTT - CIRCLA

WEBSITE: circla.co.uk

Circla is a new health and beauty brand that founder Claudia Gwinutt describes as the milk lady, but for beauty products. The company stocks a huge array of organic brands on its platform and delivers them in reusable packaging. When the customer has finished with them, instead of throwing them in the bin, Circla will come and collect them and refill them.

I finished university and didn't really know what I wanted to do, but I definitely wanted to live in London and so I joined a graduate scheme in finance. But after a while, I became disillusioned and wanted more. I'm someone who quite likes seeing and feeling things and I found that sometimes, you work on these huge projects and you're so far away from what's actually coming out the other end. I've also always been pretty passionate about sustainability and the David Attenborough Blue Planet programme had a huge impact on me.

I became hyper-aware particularly with packaging and being a bit of a beauty junkie, when I looked at my own bathroom cabinet, I realised I was a massive culprit. And I thought that there must be a better way to do things.

I remember rewriting and rewriting emails to these brands that I was already using. One of the first was Upcircle, which had always been one of my favourite brands. It was this weird, totally unprofessional email, like, "hi, my name is Claudia and we have a packaging problem and I have this solution. And would you like to talk to me?"

They were the first brand who immediately wrote back saying they loved the idea and invited me to chat to them. Then it just spiralled, with me reaching out to brands that I loved and brands approaching us, sometimes customers saying they wish we stocked certain brands. And it's got easier, but I remember that first email very clearly - it took me a long time to press the send button!

When I decided to leave my corporate job, it was quite a big decision. But once I had made up my mind from a personal perspective, I started really getting my finances in perspective, not just to invest in the business, but I knew there could be nearly two years of my life whereby having a bit of savings to pay for everything would be very helpful. It was nearly 18 months that I scrimped and saved.

I was also very fortunate. I think a lot of founders will tell you this, that building a business is about being at the right place at the right time. Someone just introducing you to that one person who has a real interest in your idea. And that is a little bit of what happened. I was at a plastic hackathon event, pitching the idea for Circla, and Sustainable Ventures were there. They have a really amazing accelerator program. And then they reached out to me afterwards to tell me they really liked me and the idea, offering pre-seed investment and an invitation to the year-long accelerator program.

That investment was used to get our first pilot up and running. We organised running a model with hotels in April of last year. We had used the funding to buy stock, the packaging and set up the infrastructure to be able to launch. Then there was this really surreal moment at the end of March. We had all the stock of shampoos, conditioners and body washes ready and packaged up in massive crates in a warehouse. The announcement about lockdown broke.

Hotels were all closed, so we couldn't deliver the product or the contracts. And I had this huge fear because no one really knew what was going to happen, or how long it was going to last for. So my parents helped me move all of the stock, because we didn't even know if I would be able to claim it from the warehouse if things got worse.

I cleared out my lounge and the next moment, I was just surrounded by shampoo bottles. And I had no idea what to do. Then it came to me - I'd built up a following and potential customers - so we decided to roll out our new milkman model for beauty products across Zones One and Two of London.

We have big plans for the future. Our immediate focus is our next investment round.

The next job is to get onboard lots of brands to become the go-to marketplace for beauty and personal care products.

And then the third target is to be able to expand outside of Zones One and Two. I'm hoping by the summer we can get to three zones of London.

When it comes to investment, we're going to be speaking to a few angel investors and small funds who invest in pre-seed businesses. This is really where the hard work comes in because it is so time-consuming, especially as a single founder.

I originally looked at doing a crowdfunding campaign and when I started looking into it, it was going to take three months of my full time to be able to get that ready. And when you're still running your business, that means three months of your time that you're not running your business.

I think one of the good things that makes me feel really comfortable at the moment is that we've got good cashflow. It's more about getting investment that lets us do things a bit quicker with maybe a little bit less risk.

We've been given the opportunity to work with a company to run an outdoor media campaign and I could obviously decide to do that now, but if it goes wrong, that's a lot of our budget for the month gone, very quickly. Whereas if we had investment, it takes a little bit of that risk away with those decisions.

The other part of it is being able to onboard the brands. At the moment, I've got about 12 in the pipeline. I could say I'm going to raise investment and bring all of them on board, but at the moment I can only do it bit by bit, because it takes a lot of work - you've got to get photography done, you've got to buy the stock, and with investment, we can just move and build that proposition out a bit quicker.

One thing that has become really obvious though, is spending money on the right things for your business, however you get investment.

I remember when I first started, I was given loads of advice saying we needed to spend a lot of budget on doing things like branding and we ended up going for it. But in hindsight, I think it was a bit too early to spend some of that money and I could have trusted my gut to do more myself, and then brought in some expertise when I was ready.

I think my biggest learning was really looking at the money and deciding what I was going to spend it on. Thinking; how do I really plan it and analyse that spend?

Whereas now, I'll get five or six quotes from different people before I do anything. And that is just a learning curve.

I also think that when you're a small business, you don't really need to be working with huge, huge agencies. There are so many amazing freelancers available. For example, when we got our website, the amazing woman who did it for us, she hadn't built a lot of Shopify websites, but explained it would take a little bit more time and in exchange, she reduced her rate for us. And I know opportunities like that are hard to find, but it is a case of networking, looking at various entrepreneur groups, speaking to lots of people, trying to get introduced to try and find that key person. I think if you just go immediately to Google, you're probably not going to get the best option.

So do your research, talk to people and find those key people that will help you get to where you want to be.

Spend your money on the things that will make a difference and be brave!

CHAPTER FOUR:

GLEN BURROWS - THE ETHICAL BUTCHER

WEBSITE: ethicalbutcher.co.uk

The Ethical Butcher is a sustainable butcher, which carefully sources its products from farmers that are focused on animal and environmental welfare. This regenerative farming system means its products taste better, are healthier and has a clear route from field to plate. "It's not just about eating good food it's about knowing where it comes from and how your choices impact both people and planet."

I studied food science at University and in the first year of my degree, I learned about a process that involved turning animal waste back into animal feed, which had caused disease mutations. And the crisis that we now know is the BSE crisis was breaking, which put me off the whole industry and specifically, eating meat. So I became vegetarian and pretty much decided I really didn't want to work in this horrible industry, so instead became a commercial photographer.

Then, twenty-five years later, in my mid-forties, I questioned myself about how I felt. What should my health be like? And am I where I should be with this? I realised that I wasn't very healthy and I didn't feel good. So I started to re-examine my options and consider how my diet might help. A couple of friends had been long-term vegetarian and had decided to make the shift to a more paleo diet as it was being called then - cutting out the grains and the sugars and eating a more natural balanced diet and they said they felt great as a result, so I decided to give it a try. For me, it was like a light bulb switching on, everything changed. All of the health problems that I was starting to develop just were magically going away. I felt better. I had more energy. And I started reading books to reacquaint myself with the health benefits of eating meat.

There was a huge amount of emphasis within the paleo movement or ethical omnivore movement, not just about eating meat, but where that comes from, how the animals were raised, and how that can affect health.

I found it increasingly difficult to find the outlets I wanted to buy from anywhere, short of going to my local farmer's market in Queens Park. And even then sometimes I was asking the person that was selling the products how the animal was raised or where it came from and I got blank looks.

I was really frustrated with the lack of transparency in the industry, and I even phoned a couple of the online butchers that I bought from regularly to say that your product is good, your packaging is terrible and your messaging's horrible and I offered to help them with my expertise. But they weren't interested and I found that frustrating.

So then I was introduced to Farshad, my co-founder, a meat trader working out of Smithfield's Market. He wanted to expand his business by crowdfunding to sell to the public. He wanted to consider the impact this new business could have and realised I was passionate about the environmental impact of meat production so he offered me some equity and we started on a journey of learning together, combining my media skills with his experience in the industry.

I did a lot of research and reading. And that has enabled me at first to at least go and speak to investors, because that was sort of the first stage of what we did - attending events where we'd meet angel investors. And we met with fund managers to try and suss things out before we went live for the first time.

We decided to go with Crowdcube in the end because it's a big platform and we'd qualified for the Enterprise Investment Scheme (EIS), which was super important. We weren't a company that was going to be founded on a rewards based system, so we knew we wanted to use a platform that offered equity. And the initial thinking for Crowdcube was that regardless of the growth of veganism, 97% of people eat meat. It was a good way of initially getting our business message out to a lot of people.

The experience of getting ready for crowdfunding, was to be honest, incredibly useful and cathartic in the same way, because we were forced to ask so many questions of the business that we hadn't even asked ourselves at that point. Even just making the deck makes you refine things like, what do you stand for? What do you want the business to look like? What are your values? What are your predictions for the business?

It's all very well asking for people to give us £350k and we'll start the business, but they want to know what we're going to do with that money. You have to answer all these questions and it makes you accountable. So it was incredibly useful, although a massive workload and very front loaded.

The main bulk of the funding was used to set us up in a unit. We took a long time to find the right kind of space and then we'd put a lot of thought and effort into how to fit the place out so that we could move in very easily.

There was a huge capital outlay on equipment and outfitting and staffing. I'm creative, but I'm always used to working under a client. So even with my own company, I wanted to find somebody who could help with that initial branding to help me narrow things down a bit. So we hired a guy called Richard Martin, who was the former CEO of Vice Media. He'd worked for Vice and had resurrected ID as a Vice channel, working on their luxury and lifestyle sector. And he was the perfect person to help the brand find purpose. And then once we defined the purpose of the brand, we could then define the strategy.

We decided early on that we wanted to appeal to an urban demographic, because most of our customers are in London. So we thought, how can we make our look appeal to someone that lives in a loft in Shoreditch rather than a farmhouse in the Cotswolds? So it was very much about forging a brand that had that traceability. The countryside would visually appeal to urban dwellers and the whole, so the very, very top line that sits above everything we do is just connecting to nature and whatever that means.

We did a huge amount of research looking at fashion brands that had rebranded in the last two years and saw, what are they doing? How are they simplifying their look? What fonts are they using and why? We were trying to think of how they've reinvented that at-home unpacking experience and how we translate that to the same guy that might walk into the Ginger Pig. How is that experience manifested in an ecosystem?

Another big part of our success was launching the Regenuary movement. Before we even launched, my brain was absolutely fizzing with information. I'd spent the summer visiting the farms and seeing the amazing transformations farmers are doing, converting old arable farms into multipack pasture systems full of wildlife. And I kept seeing posters everywhere from Domino's Pizza and KFC for Veganuary.

And it boils me. I was just so wound up by this, because these fast food restaurants have no awareness of animal welfare. I came home, had a glass of wine and wrote a slightly ranty Facebook post about it, with the word Veganuary crossed out. And it went off the charts. That first post had one million impressions and 17.5k comments. I think by the end of the month, it had been shared about 6,000 times. And then it all sort of fizzled out over the year, as these things do. And coming up to this year, again, we'd always intended to turn Reganuary into a campaign.

We weren't really ready for it this year round, but it came up in a chat with the people that look after our social media who suggested we did something to rekindle it. We decided to write a couple of posts and remind people and the whole thing sort of kicked off again.

I've had everything from outpouring of support through to death threats. and everything in between. But for me, and for the business, the thing I really enjoy discussing is the grey areas of ethics and morality, and having open and constant discussions about it.

Somebody wrote an article on Medium arguing that the most vegan thing that you could possibly eat would be grass-fed beef from a regenerative system, because if you look at the number of animal deaths per usable calorie of protein and how available it is, the death of a single cow provides one million calories that humans can use in over a thousand meals for one death. And if that cow was in a regenerative system, you probably created 40 other lives for the life of that cow because of the increased biodiversity. And then you compare that to crops grown where there's only one thing growing and everything else has been killed. The grass-fed beef comes out as having the least harm, which is the primary target of veganism - do the least harm.

We've grown very quickly. We've grown out of our space, so we're now going through the process of funding a second round on Crowdcube. We have a couple of other product ranges, which are going to sit under different brand names. We're launching white-labelled products so they're not associated with Ethical Butcher. One of the most interesting and fun things we've done is created a burger brand. We really needed to sell more mince-meat because we have a lot of surplus. So we've developed a burger brand with a separate brand name, a very different look and feel. And we've made it look like a skate brand
to appeal to a much younger audience.

We use taglines like "real meat that doesn't fuck up the planet," which is not something the Ethical Butcher would ever say. The burger buns we've made are from wheat that's been grown by a no till method and we're working with a producer to get our potatoes for the fries grown above ground, so you don't disturb the soil and release a lot of carbon. It's a carbon negative way of growing potatoes.

And then we're looking at various other products involving sourcing leather for fashion businesses, and making other products out of everything we can.

CHAPTER FIVE:
LAUREN DERRETT – WEAR 'EM OUT

WEBSITE: wearemout.co.uk

Wear 'Em Out is an innovative product that aims to create a more sustainable, environmentally-friendly product for people who period. They're reusable, durable and aim to help people feel better about their time of the month!

Most women or people with a womb get a period; it's just a part of life. Yet, it doesn't mean that you feel any less embarrassed or gross when it's your time of the month. So, there is a huge stigma around periods and I wanted to change that.

About five years ago, I started to wonder about the impacts of pads or tampons on the environment. I was shocked to find that they have a huge impact environmentally; they generate 200,000 tonnes of waste every year and they make up around 90% of plastic waste, meaning that they are harder to dispose of in an environmentally friendly way.

After doing some research, I felt guilty about having to contribute to that waste and I started wearing environmentally friendly pads out of a sense of duty; but I still felt disgusting handling them. This went on for some time until I decided to launch my own product.

Before I set about making Wear 'Em Out, my social media had grown astronomically and I had gained quite a following through other means. As a result of this I realised I could either use it for vanity numbers, or I could start doing advertisements.

However, both of the above options didn't really appeal to me. I wanted to do something tangible, and then it came to me, I thought – why not? I'm going to create something lasting for people with periods and pads.

I decided that I wanted to make a reusable pad that people wanted to wear. That it was going to be something that every woman must have. There's so much shame around periods and the impacts of menstrual products – but I wanted to create something revolutionary that people with periods would not feel embarrassed about, that was environmentally friendly and would work to break down stigma.

So, Wear 'Em Out was born. In January 2019 I began looking into creating a product of my own design; a pad that was environmentally friendly and that people with periods would feel far more comfortable using. I also wanted to make sure that this product would be made of high-quality materials. So, I decided to start looking for materials in the United Kingdom (UK).

The UK has many laws and regulations around products as their standards of care are very high. So I knew that it was the best place to start looking for materials to produce Wear 'Em Out products.

As the UK has a higher standard for what they produce, they also come with more premiums on services and because of that it is more expensive. However, it was really important for me to use the high-quality products.

After a lot of research, I found a website called "Made in Britain" and made my first investment by purchasing the directory of British Factories and Fabric Suppliers.

As soon as I downloaded it, I set to work and began emailing all of the factories and fabric suppliers about my idea, to see if they could cater towards it. This part of my journey with Wear 'Em Out was the most time-consuming (and my idea wasn't exactly a new one either), but I was determined to create something incredible.

Eventually, a designer got in touch with us, and my vision slowly started coming to life. The designer helped us look into different shapes and designs; we were passionate about making sure that the pads had a minimum amount of thickness, so that it was comfortable, but a maximum amount of absorbency. I wanted to make sure that it was a product people with periods could be confident in, where they wouldn't have to worry about bleeding out into their clothes. In my eyes, it had to be a product that suited a variety of needs; to be breathable, odourless, comfortable and environmentally friendly.

Due to the specifications, it took around a year to design, but once we had the product design, I was able to set up a team to launch the product itself in February. I made sure to surround myself with people I could trust as well – I think having that kind of support network is so important because it also meant that I had a lot of faith in my team.

I now had my team and product, so the next step was branding. I ended up shutting down my old social media accounts where I originally had such a large audience and created a new one to reflect the brand. Of course, a lot of people hated the idea of losing this following that I had built, but I wanted to make sure my product was attracting the right crowd.

It ended up working out quite well as I started building an audience and then from that I began investing more and more into building that audience up. I invested everything I had into this idea – which in total came to around £38,000. It was a lot of money, but I was determined to make this a success; and whatever I earnt from the company I just used it to reinvest back into it.

This product literally took everything I had; and I wasn't really rich to begin with. I just put everything on the table, and in a way, I think that if I hadn't put my all into it then I wouldn't have become the success I can say I am today.

One good example of a way I reinvested into the company was coaching. Not everyone is 'built' to do things and because of that there are areas of life that can be intimidating. There's no shame at all in having business coaches; I honestly think they can help you grow as a person and a business owner. Having that person to fall back on and navigate the intricacies of a business was very beneficial for me.

Social media has also been great for me, especially as a business. In terms of Instagram, I've gained a very good following on that, but social media isn't everything; I have 20,000 followers on there, but I'm prepared in case I get hacked or it gets taken away. I really believe that people should have a good mailing list to succeed with products; they are the 'hot audience' so to speak – they are the ones that have signed up to hear more from you.

So, I invested in MailChimp as well – and I have to pay for the subscribers now (as we went over the capacity that it could manage, which was in itself a great feat!) and it's something I continue to invest in. With Instagram – tomorrow I could wake up and it would all be gone, but the email subscribers means that my products would still be able to sell and we would retain our loyal customers if that happened.

I also have someone who manages the emails and similar, and this has been a time-saver for if I'm needed in other areas of the business. Due to their hard work, it has also been really effective and boosted revenue.

I've made sure that over time, I've invested in people who know what they're doing; there's things that I wouldn't attempt to do – and I wouldn't know where to start. But learning things with a new business can be so time-consuming as there's so many things you need to learn. For me, making sure that I had the right people around me that were knowledgeable helped me gain the success that I had with Wear 'Em Out.

Some people might be afraid of outsourcing; but I believe that outsourcing is where success can lie. I've had people running Facebook ads, Non-Governmental Organisation (NGO), and Instagram since March and the traction I have had from it has been amazing. I think that because of the pandemic we've also had a lot of online traction that we may not have had otherwise.

Looking at others and where they are at with their businesses has been quite inspiring for me as well. I am in a number of Facebook groups for business owners, which has been an eye-opener. It was great for me to see the growth of others and how their businesses progressed over time.

Sometimes, it was hard to know what the future looked like for my business, so because of that having other like-minded individuals that ran businesses, shared their insights, their journeys and asked questions was really helpful. From that, I could see where others were and think of the next stages for my business plan.

From being in that environment where I saw others' success and how it grew, I better understood what my next investments should be. One example is this year I will be investing in a marketing strategist for our business, who will help with the direction of our products and brand. Again, I'll be outsourcing it as I feel it's important to consistently surround yourself with knowledgeable people who can really represent your brand in the way that you want.

Looking back, I do wish I had more of a business plan as to begin with it was mostly about growth so I didn't really have a strategy. When I started out, I was just working non-stop to get the product to be what I wanted it to look like so I didn't have a set business model in mind.

Yet, I do have to thank a lot of my success to the pandemic still; I had messages from people everywhere asking if they could buy stock with Wear 'Em Out. This is because back when the pandemic began, everywhere was cleared out for sanitary products – companies were running out of stock as people were hoarding items.

People were just desperate, so they ended up coming to us to buy pads instead. From there, people tried our products and wanted to continue using us; they tried and tested our products and saw it was effective, comfortable and had the benefit of being environmentally friendly. So we knew that after they had tried it once it was what they wanted to continue using.

The pandemic paired with all the investing I had used for social media meant that we blew up in terms of popularity. People flocked to this new, innovative pad that was comfortable, durable, odourless, easy to handle and was environmentally friendly.

I think that as people during the pandemic also learned more about the environment, they were more keen to invest in our products. Altogether, I think all these little things were contributors to the success that we had with

Wear 'Em Out.

For me though, most of the success came from my investments – I made sure that I repeatedly made choices and investments for the good of the company. I wanted to make sure that I was accurately building the brand that I wanted to put out into the world.

CHAPTER SIX

LISA LAWSON - DEAR GREEN COFFEE

WEBSITE: deargreencoffee.com

Lisa Lawson is the founder of Dear Green Coffee, a sustainable coffee brand which has recently won a B Corp Status and is celebrating ten years! Lisa's company is now one of Scotland's biggest green coffee roasters. The company is based in Scotland and Glasgow and their coffee is unmatched!

I learnt how to roast coffee when I was backpacking in Australia and New Zealand. I spent three years in total travelling and enjoyed every second of it! Roasting coffee held a special place in my heart as I continued to travel and then when I eventually settled in Glasgow, I hoped I could continue to do just that.

However, when I came to Glasgow, I found that there wasn't anywhere I was able to work and roast coffee. So, I settled here for a few years but ran into some bad experiences with the employers I had.

I had always loved coffee and enjoyed roasting it. Eventually, it got to the stage where I realised that I just had to bite the bullet to start my own coffee business. Otherwise, it would end up being one of those things that would always bother me and I would spend the rest of my life thinking what if?

I decided to set up Dear Green Coffee in late 2011. Once I had decided to set up a business, I didn't really have much in mind on how to do it – I didn't have a business plan, I didn't seek out investors, I didn't have a mentor. In some ways, it was like flying by the seat of your pants!

I didn't really have a clue what I was doing, but I was very passionate about creating something incredible and I knew that would guide me to where I needed to go with the business.

So, once I had the idea to set up Dear Green Coffee, I was very lucky in a way. This is because from my time backpacking, I already knew how to make my own coffee and I had great customer service skills. Which meant I had just one important thing left, which was seeking out coffee suppliers and production companies.

However, there were not many suppliers and partners that I could choose from to start producing and roasting coffee – especially green raw coffee. So, we were very limited in where we could go.

I ended up settling on suppliers that I knew from another source. I approached them first and they gave me supplies for a while to get started with making the coffee.

After setting up, coffee had suddenly started gaining momentum everywhere – people were seeking out specialty coffee – cafes, importers and coffee roasteries had started opening up everywhere. Again, I was quite lucky as I started selling coffee on that curve.

Dear Green Coffee then began to grow just as the obsession with coffee did. We became more spoilt for choice, and both suppliers and importers began to approach us. We went from being very limited in our options on where to go to being surrounded by them.

It was amazing how much things changed as well, as coffee became popular. I got myself a coffee roaster, then more and more products came up on our radar and we were able to start expanding!

As our company began to expand, we started investing in various different parts of it. There was the brewing equipment, commercials, bristle machines, grinders, etc. Technology had begun to advance just as coffee grew more popular, so we wanted to make sure that we knew about any new machinery, and the changes in the technical side of coffee making.

We wanted to make sure that our coffee was the best, whilst still supporting our wholesale customers as much as possible.

It was great in lots of ways, as I learnt a lot about coffee itself – the process, quality control, visiting coffee farms and meeting the people who make the coffee beans.

The process of coffee itself is very fascinating – a lot of people don't know that a coffee bean is actually a seed that is dried, roasted and then ground up to make coffee! It was an incredible experience seeing the process of it all and how it then ended up coming into our hands.

We cared a lot about making our coffee as natural and as ethical as possible. So, when we eventually decided on where to source our coffee from and what our values were, it was also the perfect time to apply for a B Corp Status.

B Corp is short for Benefit Corp and it means that your company doesn't put profit first (although, you need to be profitable in at least some way, to make sure that your company is sustainable and can be ongoing). We achieved the B Corp status recently and it really does feel great to be certified with it.

I was always passionate about making coffee, but our company is now so much more than that. We want to protect our social environment and the planet and so we ticked all the boxes in terms of ethics when it came to applying for a B Corp status. Knowing that your company was founded in integrity and is part of a larger community who really cares about the world and environment is such a heart-warming feeling. Our coffee proves that we can have something in sustainable and ethical origins – even if it can be hard to make that change.

I do think there's so much more to businesses than just the above though. When you don't try to find the cheapest products and charge extortionate prices for it, you get a better response from your customer base. It's important to care about your community around you, and look after your staff – and this is what I believe made our company grow faster.

Adjusting is so important in business as well. We had a small espresso bar before COVID hit, but that had to close down, so we lost a huge part of our business.

COVID changed so many companies' outlooks – you needed to change your view of how to operate in order to survive. So, we ended up going from a wholesale business to an online one.

Luckily for us, we had already put a lot of time and research into search engine optimisation (SEO) and we had a really good ecommerce website set up. From there, we were able to push out our subscriptions and develop our newsletters. We just took the time to adjust the best we could, and pivot into this new way of life.

When we made the change to online, we ended up having less staff and more coffee. It was hard in some ways, changing from retail to wholesale is no easy task! Yet, we just worked as hard as we could, knowing that we had the tools to continue to be successful.

So, we planned – we looked at projects, updated processes, used quality control. We spent the time that we had investing in the other areas of the business. At the same time though, all of us were looking forward to when things started reopening.

One thing which we were excited for was the Glasgow Coffee Festival, which our company runs. We hire venues and have businesses come to us from all over the UK and some international guests – it's a great experience for coffee lovers everywhere!

Last year we couldn't run the festival because of Covid, so we had to adjust the best we could instead. As I said before, adjusting is so important in the business world – you need to do it to survive. So, instead of hosting the festival and booking venues last year, we instead took the festival to the streets.

People would buy a ticket and get a discount for fifty different cafes over the course of ten days and it honestly worked out so well! So well, in fact, that we're probably going to do something like that again this year!

Right now, we're just trying to focus on adjusting to what life will be like in the future – thinking ahead, monitoring what's happening with our coffee bar, looking at our customer base, making sure they're happy, branding, packaging, etc.

For me, in terms of investing, branding has been so important, but if I could give any advice to any new entrepreneurs, I would say that investing in everything else is just as needed – packaging, good people, good equipment and making sure that what you do is ethical and sustainable in the long-run.

Another piece of advice I would give anybody who is wanting to work for themselves is to do something you have a passion for – passion helps you to keep going no matter where you are in your journey!

CHAPTER SEVEN:

BOYOWA OLUGBO - STENNAH & HOPE DISPLACED FRAGRANCES

WEBSITE: stennahandhope.co.uk

Stennah and Hope was launched in 2009 by Boyowa Olugbo and from there they have created a home fragrance and toiletries brand that is completely and utterly natural. In 2012 Boyowa launched a wholesale brand and this year he is launching a social enterprise.

It's been a long, hard journey to get to the point that I'm at now, but it's definitely been a fulfilling one. Stennah and Hope is an award winning bespoke candle and toiletry manufacturer.

We offer vegan, organic and natural bespoke products. We're also quite different to traditional companies as we don't mass produce thousands and thousands of products. However, we do cater to some high-street brands and provide products for special events and holidays like Christmas.

My journey started in 2007, at the time I was making candles and giving them out to family and friends for Christmas. Everyone really, really loved them and then turned around and said to me *these are amazing! You should definitely turn this into a business!* So, I decided to think on it for a while.

I decided there was no harm in trying it out, I was in the music industry as a songwriter and a music producer, but the world of music was changing so fast. It had got to a point where it felt like I couldn't be as creative as I wanted to be, and I was feeling disheartened with the industry as a whole.

As that industry was changing so much, I had wanted to try something new anyway so I began making candles. Then, in 2008 I got some investments from a few friends and we spent a year putting something together with it all.

As I had been thinking of doing something new, I also went back to university around the same time to do a teaching qualification. So I was learning how to teach whilst making the candles. I was still somewhat in the music industry, but it was very quiet overall, so my focus was elsewhere.

In 2009, me and my friends had been working on the candles together and we had the opportunity to launch them with Space NK in May. It took off quite well with them as fifty-five stores ended up having this candle range that we had made.

The candles themselves were amazing. We had incredible artwork on the candles and if you had the entire collection all the artwork blended together.

We launched exclusively for six months only, and it went really well. So, in the first year it was just me making them in my kitchen and then the next we were everywhere. But, we didn't have any idea what we were doing – especially with marketing.

In fact, I didn't even know what a purchase order was until the first one landed in my inbox. We would get the purchase order together, and then make it, and deliver it, then before I knew it we got the next, and the next, and the next...

It was a nightmare... It was a great nightmare because we were picking up so much traction, but it was a nightmare where I didn't really know what I was doing. So that feeling continued for about six months, until we decided to do reed diffusers as well.

I actually bought a reed diffuser for my house at the time and that inspired us to start branching out into different fragrances, like reed diffusers, rather than just sticking to candles.

We then realised that home fragrances were just going to be a constant investment. You've got to make sure you get new products, new scents, new fragrances, new designs… It's just an endless investment really.

So, my two investor friends at the time told me that they would hand over the company to me. I was grateful for everything they had done but it came to a point where they couldn't invest any more money into it.

It was alright though in my eyes, I felt like I was able to manage it all – but from there it became more difficult. Candles were becoming more of a seasonal thing from September – January. So, because of that I would have a massive gap in between spring and summer where I barely had an income. So, from 2012 - 2013 I just realised this way of working wasn't sustainable and that I had to do something.

At the time, I kind of realised that I was selling candles to people and places, but maybe it was time to make candles for brands instead.

I thought about everything that I'd learned over the last few years in terms of packaging, fragrances and glass printing – and then I just realised I could put that as a wrap-around service for other brands.

After all, if you think about it, candles for a lot of brands are seen more as accessories. For them, it's something that they're adding on top of the other services they offer. As a result of that, they do not necessarily have the time to go and put it all together.

So I just thought well, I can do that for them, I can put it all together and deliver it. I just need to get the ball rolling.

I decided to start by going to trade shows and I would identify which brands I wanted to work with; in particular ones that were focused on natural and organic products.

Between 2012 and 2013 veganism wasn't such a big thing, but there were plenty of places that were interested in natural, organic products. So, I just approached the brands that I liked and was able to talk to a lot of people.

During the first four trade shows I attended, I got two commercial orders and it just went from there. One brand recommended me to another, and I just kept trying to build up my reputation with one company and brand at a time.

I wasn't making a lot of money, but understanding the process, how to invoice, or anything like that. I was literally learning every step of the way – but although I didn't know all of those things, I still knew how to make a good candle. The product itself was great; so I knew that things would pick up eventually.

Then, things did pick up – I built every part of my business one step at a time as it continued to grow. Now I'm at a point where we've got big plans for the future and we're partnered with some really upmarket hotels, spas and skincare ranges that use candles.

It was all word-of-mouth recommendations to get to that point though, and we've just built it up one step at a time.

It's crazy from where it started though, because looking back I have come so far with this company. For example, with my first order I was living in a two bedroom flat, where there was about 800 – 900 candles and it was a complete nightmare.

There were candles everywhere; boxes in the passageway, my son's bedroom, in the kitchen. Now, it's incredible to think that we're in a space of nearly over 4000 square feet. We've come a long way and although it's been nine years in the making, it's great to think of how the business has come along in that time.

When the business first launched I didn't know what I was doing, I had no idea about investment and everything I learnt, I learnt the hard way. To anyone that might feel as though they are in a similar boat, I would advise two different ways of going about it.

Personally, I never had any outside investment – other than initial help from my friends – I did it with my own money, credit cards, overdrafts, loans, you name it. But I did it that way because I knew that I could sustain that and fulfil it, I never had any trouble in keeping up with any of that.

However, if I was to start all over again I would do it another way. One of my mentors once told me that I was trapped in my business, and that is exactly what happens when you're investing everything into it. You are the business, you're doing everything and it gets to a place where you can't get out of it. All of my personal assets were completely tied up with the business and it was a dangerous way to go about it for the rest of my life.

So I would recommend getting someone else to run certain parts of the business, to free up your time for other things. Admittedly, I wouldn't change my journey to get to this point as honestly there's so many things that I've learnt along the way.

In terms of investment as well it's so complex. There are people that I've spoken to where their life is spent talking to investors and trying to sort out their kick-starters or crowdfunding campaigns. Their whole life is just setting up the campaigns and that's what they see as a success. It's very different to how I got to where I am.

I'm now lucky enough though to be at a point where I'm analysing what I can outsource and what I can get someone else to do. I'm trying to outsource as much as I can although, I think there's things that you could never outsource – to me it's still hard outsourcing because I've spent so long in the business managing it all alone.

The next exciting thing that we're doing is launching displacedfragrances.com It's come about because we get inundated with people who just want to start candle brands, especially in the last eight months since the lockdown has happened. Being a candle manufacturer, I always wanted to launch one, but there's no fun in it anymore because well, there's just so many nowadays!

So, I wanted to do something else, something that is different. For me, I've always been very much into music, education and fragrances. Education is a massive part of my life, and I spent ten years teaching 16 – 19 year olds that were quite hard to reach.

I worked with kids that had been expelled, or hard to reach in the eyes of society and mainstream schools. But, I really enjoyed it and I really identified with them.

Yet, I couldn't draw the best out of them. So, I thought maybe there was a different way to reach them? So, that's when I decided to set up the centre. The centre has candle-making classes, and then we would be on the shop floor with them, helping them manage it, market it and they would have their identity on it.

From there we were able to expand into the community and help them realise their ambitions. A lot of the time when you're seen as though you're on the bottom rung of society, there's just certain things that you feel that you can't achieve because you've been marked as less. So this place that I've created, it's really exciting – it's scary – but it's exciting.

After that, we're just going to be building it into a bigger platform, where young people can come and have access to graphics, music and most importantly education for them all.

This process helps people find and realise their dreams in a different way, which you may not necessarily get from a mainstream form of education. These people will realise that they don't have to go to university to do incredible things (although, I hope it helps those who want to go to university realise that they can). Instead it will really help them put their life into perspective and have more accountability, we also have mentors and coaches for them that helps them to figure out what they really want to do with their lives.

Obviously, this all started with candles – but it's grown into so much more than that. With the candles, it's going to be giving finance, education and the young people what they really need. It's like a new path towards a better future. Of course, I don't expect anyone to decide to make candles for the rest of their lives, but they'll come into this and they'll have their "eureka!" moment and realise what it is they want out of life.

Then, with every candle we sell instead of just candles or just another brand, it's helping people come one step closer to their dreams. Which for me, has been the best-case scenario for my business.

I think that my parting words to any future entrepreneurs is to just make sure that you're doing something you can do every day, be humble and don't be afraid to do things that can give back to the community.

CHAPTER EIGHT:
SARAH JORDAN - YOU UNDERWEAR

WEBSITE: youunderwear.com

Sarah Jordan is the founder and CEO of You Underwear, which is an ethical and sustainable underwear brand that's trying to make a difference. For every pair that is purchased, two pairs are bought for developing communities.

We are a sustainable and ethical underwear brand that's made from organic cotton and everything we make is sustainably sourced. We really believe in the principles of fair pay and treating workers through the supply chain, and we also donate two pairs of underwear to Smalls for All for every one that someone buys. Smalls for All is a Scottish Charity that collects and distributes underwear to vulnerable women and children across Africa and the UK.

Overall, we're trying to source sustainably and give back to the communities that need it. However, believe it or not, I didn't set out to have a business!

I travelled to volunteer in Uganda in 2016. It was through something called the Uganda marathon programme, which was a run but it also supported working and living in local communities. So, I was just helping them with different projects.

One of the groups that I worked with, were female entrepreneurs, who were making sanitary towels and nappies and really struggling with it as a business. Due to that, they were trying to make a name for themselves in the community, but as a small start-up business they couldn't get it off the ground and wasn't sure why.

Whilst there, we managed to work out that the reason they couldn't sell them was because the women didn't have any underwear. So, there was no point in having a sanitary towel because if you didn't have underwear you couldn't do anything with it. For me, it was really shocking that this was the reality behind it.

Underwear is just a fundamental product in our everyday lives – it's literally the first thing you put on in the morning and such a basic necessity that you take for granted. If you don't have underwear or sanitary products it can have such a massive impact on your life – especially as a woman.

For women, this isn't just about health and hygiene issues either, there is the risk of violence, safety, and even not having access to education. There were girls that were missing a week of school every month because of their periods; when girls started their periods (between 9 – 10) they wouldn't be able to go to school, older women wouldn't be able to go to work, and were excluded from their local communities.

So, from when a girl first started their period, they were instantly set on such a different path from the boys in their community. It already had an impact on their future, as they couldn't even go to school. It just really stuck with me, because again it was just something that was so simple. Why is it still a problem?

We know about period poverty here in the UK and it's the same, so you need the products but you also need the underwear. So, when I came back from that trip it was just constantly on my mind and I really wanted to do something about it. Why can't women have access to underwear? Then I essentially started looking into it as a problem and trying to solve that.

As I was looking into it, I started viewing different underwear brands and how they were manufactured. I found that cotton underwear is better for you because it's more breathable as a natural fibre. Yet, conventional cotton is actually really bad, it pollutes the environment, isn't waterproof and is made with lots of pesticides. There's a huge issue behind the scenes in the cotton farming industry and again, I was left feeling really shocked at what I had learnt.

In India, it's really bad as well, in the cotton farming industry cotton farmers were committing suicide at a rate of one every thirty minutes. I was horrified, it was just such a huge problem that nobody was really aware of. Then, looking at the fashion industry as a whole it's not very nice in terms of its working practices and how much it pays people. Especially women and the way it treats them.

Eventually, it got to a point where I just put two and two together and decided that I was going to do something.

I decided that I was going to create underwear that was sustainable and create a business that could support itself. Not just by charity donations, or something that was one off, but something that would be around for a long time and was sustainable. So, I needed to create a business that would be able to support itself.

In particular, I needed to source sustainably, so right from the start I wanted to use organic cotton, as it polluted the environment far less, and would help support the farmers themselves.

It was quite a journey going from my trip, to then turning it into a business. At the time, I was kind of familiar with how charity models work and the pros and cons of that, to then working with local partners on the ground.

So I knew that I needed to explore how I could get the underwear out to these rural communities and support them. Then thinking about it in business terms, I needed to make something that could be sustainable in the long-term. In particular, I wanted to make sure the products themselves were sourced as ethically as possible.

I actually consider myself quite lucky as I found a sustainable and ethical manufacturer that I could use quite quickly.

When it came to the Indian cotton farmer issues, it was a friend that informed me of it all. He runs an organic clothing business in India and was telling me about the issues that the farmers face. So, when I learnt about these issues, I knew I had to do what I could to help. So, he put me in touch with this manufacturer and they've got all kinds of certifications when it comes to making the cotton.

They only use certified organic cotton, and it's all Fairtrade, so because of that, it pays people right the way through the supply chain. They had additional certifications under legislation laws which showed that they gave additional support to workers such as providing them with education, transport and supporting the rest of their families.

It was great knowing that I was investing in something that had transparency as one of the other problems in fashion is the people you're working with via the company are alright, but they're outsourcing most of the work. However, the manufacturer we work with does either own or work with local communities who have the cotton farms. So we've got visibility in terms of having that reassurance. Although it has been hard, especially given that you can't travel because of COVID.

I was really keen to find a partner in manufacturing who had the same values, and I actually went out in 2019 to see how our underwear was made. It was quite an enlightening process, because you think it's simple and it's not. If you don't visit these places as well, how do you know what the conditions are like? It's part of a much wider issue I think.

In terms of my background before I started out, it was nothing to do with manufacturing, and because of that everything I've learned since then was totally new. So search engines and social media have been invaluable.

When I came back from Uganda I had also broken my leg, so I had to spend the next year on crutches. On the bright side, it gave me the time to start working on this underwear brand and create something. It took a year to turn it into a business though, because I wanted to help people and places; not hinder them.

So after getting the manufacturing, the model, the funding, the partner and the charity to help us donate, it left me with trying to get the products sampled.

In the end, we made a crowdfunding campaign, so that's how we were able to get over the first hurdle of funds, then we did another crowdfunding campaign in 2017 just for Christmas. We managed to raise an incredible amount, which gave us enough to get our products out there.

With the products, the biggest problem with that side of the business is the cash flow. You have to buy the products upfront, then you resell them, so you're constantly investing at the start and then trying to repay that by selling the items essentially.

So that in itself was a journey – the crowdfunding we actually thought about in the summer, but then decided that just before Christmas was a better option as people tend to be more generous and they may want to purchase the underwear for gifts.

However, we did end up hitting a bump in the road, as the products themselves didn't end up arriving until two days before Christmas – and we had already committed ourselves to fulfilling the orders for presents. So, I spent the last two days before Christmas that year hand delivering the under-wear to everybody that backed us! Luckily they loved it, but it was an absolute nightmare at the time – I guess it was great for the consumers to see what they were buying into, but two days before Christmas… Well, it was a little rushed.

In terms of fashion as well, we were definitely in slow fashion, which takes a lot longer, as it's harder to get the items. We manufacture in India because that's where most of the organic cotton has grown, so we have less of an impact by bringing the final items in.

In 2018 we went live with the website, just over three years ago. We made the crowdsourcing back through the sales and since then it's been a kind of circular model in terms of investing. I pour a lot into the business – to buy the next set of products and then develop, sell, and reinvest.

It was also a great lesson in a lot of ways too – when people think of crowdfunding, whether it's Kickstarter or Crowdcube, they should think of it for the actual investment rather than a product swap and that you don't need to raise millions or hundreds or even thousands – but actually, just having that buffer for cash flow is really indispensable.

With crowdfunding though, it's often not quite what people think. I think a lot of people view it as a silver bullet for free money; whereas it's much more than that. It's a really hardcore marketing campaign for that period of like 30 days, or however long it's live. You're constantly chasing people and the product itself isn't on their radar like it is yours. So, they'll say they support you and they mean it, and then the deadline comes and you're more focused on it then them.

In hindsight though, that was what got us enough to get those products out there and start moving. You don't need millions – and that's the kind of business model that I've had. Growing steadily, partly through need.

Pouring funds into it has definitely helped though. Of course, I've never had a huge amount to invest in the business, but I've been trying to grow it sustainably and organically.

The product has also received a lot of word of mouth and recommendations. Although we have a website and social media with SEO, we've been trying really hard to make sure the people purchasing the products are looking for organic cotton underwear and we don't have a big budget to market to everyone, we can't.

Although, as I worked in the charity sector for a while I suppose that was one of the advantages that I had, money was always tight. We always had small budgets, we always had limited resources but at the end of the day that was what made you very creative and made you analyse where you're spending every penny.

You have to justify every penny – I don't have a huge amount of money to spend, so I'm going to invest it to the best of my ability as wisely as I can However, the products are the biggest challenge because obviously that's where the biggest chunk of cash that we spend is.

We're growing in range though – and we actually had a really good year in 2020. I think there's been a shift in people supporting small businesses, local businesses and sustainable ones. Also, being at home and wanting comfy underwear kind of coincided, so we've been really lucky and now it's just about growing our range.

We want to be as size inclusive as possible, so we want more sizes coming in, more colours and more styles of underwear for people to choose from. In fact, when I started I didn't even realise how many different styles of underwear there were for women (there's at least 25 different types of knickers)! We've also got sizes from 6 – 22 and that's a lot to have for just a small business.

I'm also very excited about a collaboration with a designer in Nairobi to get some funky prints out there. At the moment our core colours are neutral with black, white, grey and a couple of skin tones. However, the new designs are really bright and they have amazing prints. On top of that we thought if we're going to go colourful, let's go really colourful! We want to try and bring the origin back to the business in Africa as well – as that's what really led me on this journey.

On top of that, we've created a range that has been designed by local girls for the younger girls, as a lot of underwear products don't suit their needs. So, some of my friends with their daughters told us what they wanted and we did the patterns for them and put the designs together. We've just launched those and it's great to see that we're increasing our range to more and more people.

Doing all of the above also meant that we were able to register for a B Corp status as well to solidify how much of a sustainable and ethical business we are. I actually think consumers are going to more actively look for B Corp businesses now as there's a bigger societal change towards ethical products.

If I could offer any advice to someone, it would be to take inspiration from the things you see around you. I was really shocked and appalled at all these things that I learnt, and I wanted to create something that could change things for the better.

CHAPTER NINE:

KRESSE WESSLING, MBE - ELVIS & KRESSE

WEBSITE: elvisandkresse.com

Kresse Wesling is half of the legendary accessories brand Elvis &
Kresse. They use damaged, decommissioned London fire brigade hoses,
failed parachutes and off-cut leather from Burberry to make their bags,
belts and purses. They also give 50% of all their profits to the Fire
Fighter's Charity.

I moved to the UK in 2004 and brought with me something of an obsession with rubbish. I spent a lot of time at the British Library, researching waste statistics. Most of this information is now accessible on a smartphone but the Business and IP centre at the British Library is still an incredible asset for the curious.

I was horrified to discover that in 2004 the UK sent 100 million tonnes of waste to landfill. I couldn't imagine how or where this truly astounding amount was being buried. It didn't make sense to me; so I started visiting waste transfer stations, recycling centres and ultimately visiting as many landfill sites as I could.

Although landfills are chaotic, smelly and messy there are also incredibly beautiful and pristine materials coming in by the lorry load. We now lament 'single use plastics' but I was consistently seeing things that had never been used. There were so many industrial by-products that had never really seen the light of day, it was astounding.

One day, something in particular that caught my eye – and although it could have been anything in hindsight – I happened to lock eyes with a fire hose. A short time later I had a chance meeting two people working on sustainability with the London Fire Brigade. They directed me to their hose and line shop, where hoses go to be repaired or decommissioned. Their rooftop was covered in glorious coils of rich red hoses. I felt immediately that each and every 22 metre hose could not be abandoned, I was certain they had so much left to give.

Each hose has its own life-saving history, it didn't seem dignified to let it languish in landfill, so I took it home with me and we let it percolate with us for a while, trying all the time to work out what the next best life for this material would be.

Elvis and I then went back to the library to attempt to become fire-hose experts. We wanted to know everything about it: melting point, breaking point, durability… in order to solve a problem you need to really understand the problem. We had no outcome in mind, no particular product. It was our research, it was the nature of the hose itself which led us to transform it into a range of belts, bags and wallets and launch a luxury brand.

At the time, there were no website building tools like Shopify or Squarespace which meant that Elvis had to learn to code to build our first website using Dreamweaver software.

We were really, really early into the online movement and we also had very limited production, we only made belts for most of our first year. We then financed our first production run by making one prototype bag and telling everyone we knew about it. We pre-sold enough bags to make a first run of 800 pieces. We were amazed that there was so much faith in our small business, and our one and only bag. Just think about it... Kickstarter was founded in 2009 but we did our own analogue version of a Kickstarter campaign years earlier!

Since this first production run we have been financed entirely by sales and organic growth. The business that we built is based on what is in our hearts, and how we would like the world to be.

We didn't just rescue fire-hose though, it was the first material we collected, but soon after we started, other materials followed. We started collecting old office textiles, parachute silk, coffee sacks, 1970s printed tablecloths... Those were probably the wildest, as both the patterns and the colours couldn't be from any other decade.

We had a knack for finding interesting materials and meeting the lovely people who really didn't want to waste them and had been hoarding them. We also found lots of industrial partners too, like Costa Coffee; we collected their coffee sack waste for years, transforming it into reusable shopping bags. Rescue is at the core of everything we do - whether it is the lining, the packaging, our furniture... we make everything from waste and everything ourselves. Even our business cards are made from air traffic control flight strips from the National Air Traffic Service!

Also, we donate 50% of our profits to charity. From the fire-hose range 50% of the profits are donated to the Fire Fighters Charity, which means we have always had a great relationship with these stakeholders. It also means that finding new partners and collaborators is in our DNA.

When we started looking at leather in 2010, we had some great early suppliers who helped us to get started. Then, in 2013 we were approached by Burberry. They appreciated our novel solution for leather off-cuts and we started a long conversation which eventually led to the launch of a long-term partnership with the Burberry Foundation in 2017.

Over the years we have witnessed a consistent shift in the fashion industry. People are gradually moving away from fast fashion and the linear economy of take-make-waste. It is lovely to see more and more people buying slowly and thoughtfully as they consider how their buying decisions impact people and the planet. However, this shift is happening way too slowly. The real impact for us has come not from us, but from what our work has unleashed… from stakeholders and collaborators that have also made huge changes, from the incredible progress that our charity partners have made and from the hundreds of young entrepreneurs we have inspired; even though we are a small company we can have an impact way beyond our size just by choosing to be generous and transparent.

We have grown consistently, every year, and interestingly this growth has continued through the pandemic; the shift to online obviously worked for us as a primarily online business but we also received a steady flow of calls and emails from customers expressing their support. The pandemic made them think even harder about their purchasing power, they were keen to spend their money in more sustainable ways because they wanted their money to mean something.

When customers invest in us, they are investing in a whole host of good things; we rescue and reuse materials, we donate 50% of our profits, we are a Living Wage employer, we are a Certified Social Enterprise and Founding UK B Corp, we run an apprenticeship program, we run on renewable energy, and we treat all our own sewage on site, just using the power of nature. Fundamentally, when people have the time to do their research, if they can stop and think about the kind of world they want to live in and the kind of businesses they want to support, this shifts customers to businesses like ours.

There is so much more to be done, though, and I think that in terms of making changes that can improve our long-term trajectory, we need to invest more as a civil society, globally, in institutions with real power. Think of an Environmental Protection Agency that was at the heart of policy decisions, taxation, and fines. It doesn't make sense to us that private companies can make any kind of profit when it is at the expense of the environment, or when people are exploited in the process. Our company is a Certified Social Enterprise and B Corp, but I want to see a world where businesses have to put a logo on their website that literally says they are destroying the planet. We need more ways to show that other businesses are unethical or unsustainable.

Imagine a supermarket with an Unfair trade aisle…

It is always amazing to us, to think back to where we started. We began our business in a shared house in Brixton. We were making belts in our bedroom and for a long time there was a sewing machine beside the bed. Then we moved into a conservatory, then a garage, then our first in a series of larger workshops. And now we are based on a farm where we are building our own workshop from straw bales, a highly insulated building that stays warm in the winter and cool in the summer.

Everything has been self-funded and as a result of that it has taken a long time for us to get to where we are now. We didn't go down the investment route, which has made our journey slow but it has also allowed us to develop completely in line with the strong values that permeate everything we do and all our decision making.

There were investors that came to see us in the early years, but none of them were right for us… they either wanted us to raise prices, lower our donations or opt for cheaper manufacturing. Had we accepted any of these early investment offers we don't think we would have been able to go on this incredibly impactful and creative journey, consistently widening our scope and rescuing many more materials. It would have taken away the independence that has allowed us to be values led, and be ourselves.

Are there things I wish we had done differently? Absolutely, that said, I don't think I would go back and change anything. I am really pleased with where we are and any one of those things that we decided to change could lead to very different outcome. We are a product of our successes as well as our failures and omissions.

One of the questions we are asked all of the time is about our commitment to donations. This was a snap decision. We were looking at a stunning stack of fire hoses that the fire department was going to throw away and in that moment, back in 2005, I promised to take it all. I also promised that if I was successful, I would give them half of any profits. At the time, the two guys I talked with thought this was hysterical and probably that they would never see me again. None of us knew what would happen, but an incredible partnership with both the London Fire Brigade and the Fire Fighters Charity ensued.

The way we started the business has come to embody who we are. Our model consists of three simple actions:

· We Rescue
· We Transform
· We Donate

We have also discovered that the saying "the more you give, the more you receive" is true. Not only has goodwill been our greatest engine of growth but it is emotionally fulfilling for us and our whole team too. I really do wish more businesses would try it.

Let me be very clear. We do not think of our donations as a sacrifice. They are really the least that we can do. Human beings are just one species and we can't exist on our own, or without each other. We exist in communities and rely on one another. We rely on the earth and its resources. Every individual, every business and every government needs to think how their actions can make everything better for everyone and for the environment. Unfortunately, these aren't the laws that govern us… we don't have these legal structures – but it's how I believe that we should operate.

The B Corp movement in the UK and the US is growing incredibly quickly to the extent that they cannot certify businesses fast enough. This is wonderful news but we're only a small portion of the business world and I think we need to move faster overall if we're going to survive.

In terms of what's next, we are constantly working on four or five materials that we know we can rescue. We have also just completed an incredible R&D project with a team from Queen Mary University. Together we have developed a renewably powered micro-forge, to enable safe, cheap and widespread recycling of aluminium. We are just at the point of open-sourcing this technology and sharing all of our research.

Our solar-powered forge will help us collect aluminium cans; in the UK we litter 16 million of these each year into our public spaces. This litter issue also has an impact on biodiversity with a devastating impact on the small mammal population. We're incredibly proud of how we've been able to make this project work and what the future holds.

Advice for a new small business? Solve problems and give back. I can guarantee that whatever you give will come back to you tenfold.

CHAPTER TEN

PHILL KALLI - FILL REFILL CO.

WEBSITE: fillrefill.co

Phillip Kalli is the founder of Fill Refill Co who formulate, design, make & deliver closed loop cleaning, laundry & personal care products to zero waste stores, refill shops & conscious businesses around the UK. They also supply direct to consumer in a closed loop, taking back packaging to wash, reuse & refill. It was also the first company to pioneer a way to circularise supply of household products using the milkman model nationally, working closely with Milk & More to get rinse and return product onto doorsteps (and the empties back to the factory for refilling) since June 2020.

You might be surprised, but I'm no chemist. I went to Chelsea College of Art and then studied English Literature at Bristol University. I worked for a music magazine and then managed a rock'n'roll band for about five years - we signed to EMI, toured a whole bunch, released an LP before EMI got taken over by Guy Hands and his consortium and it all fell apart.

At the end of all that I had to think hard about what I wanted to do next. I'm really close to my dad and I was keen to understand more about what he was doing. He has a PhD in chemistry and never really worked a day for anyone else. He was brave enough to try and start his own manufacturing company back in the 80s. Back then, as a handsome young chemist, he'd come up with a new professional laundry product formulation that turned out to be revolutionary. It saved a lot of water, energy and time. He was determined to find a way to make it himself, taking on far bigger companies along the way. He'd run the same business for a long time... making bulk detergents. He's always been passionate about making the most efficient products possible and finding ways to supply them to independent laundries around the UK.

He asked me if I wanted to join him to see what he did and I decided to give it a go. I soon realised that he'd never done any marketing, branding or advertising. He'd never really considered anything other than making the best product he could - which I really admired.

So I joined him, with the understanding that I'd give it a year or two and see how we got on. I enjoyed those first two years getting to know what we did, meeting a lot of passionate people who enjoyed working with my Dad. It was clear there were a lot of things being done well, but there was room for a lot of change! I had an interest in sustainability and was motivated by how we could be more responsible with the products that we make & supply.

Back in 2011 I read something about a Canadian store called 'The Soap Dispensary' - a good looking store that was offering refill of various household products to help eliminate plastic waste. The soap wasn't made by the store owners, it was coming for all kinds of different local suppliers, but it was always available in bulk.

I fixated on that idea and couldn't let it go. It seemed so obvious and so important.

I looked into whether there was anything similar in the UK which led me to find the first Unpackaged store in Clerkenwell, run by Catherine Conway. I was mesmerised with the concept At the time, it seemed logical and radical and I wanted to see how we could get involved.

I approached the store in Clerkenwell about making products for them and just felt that we could do something. We had the facilities and I had this idea that we could turn what we already do into something that supplies direct to consumers in bulk, to eliminate all the single use plastic that traditionally surrounded the household cleaning & laundry sector.

I spent a long time thinking about how we could go about doing it best, I still do!

My Dad and I even approached the bank with an idea to open our own store, where we made all the products... They really went for the idea, but we had enough to handle with getting all the formulations, production and packaging ready so we never saw it through in that guise (for now anyway).

I had another idea to offer cleaning and laundry products from an old ice cream van that would pitch up in the car parks of supermarkets, guerrilla style. As we had the feeling that supermarkets simply weren't willing to change to a refill model back then!

I just thought it was a really cool idea but then life got in the way for a while. The whole time though, I was perfecting this idea. I scribbled out what became the logo on a bit of paper. We had a concept, we thought about the manufacturing capabilities, but then it was just about asking other questions and finding the answers.

Like how do we improve it over time? How do we get all the products right?

It was hard, because sometimes it was like you were going around in circles and there was no real blueprint on how to go about what we had. Then came the loop, which eventually we managed to close.

Closing a loop means making something sustainable in the long term and one way I managed to make this work is from my friend Hamish, who runs a company called Planet Minimal. I met him a couple of years ago and he helped me to set up the loop. Hamish was really passionate about building a business around electric vehicles and sustainability, so he was great to have on board (I would like to add that the loop isn't particularly glamorous, but it holds the key to the whole process of our products working).

Hamish then managed to get a huge warehouse space and we delivered the products to him in two giant 1000 litre intermediate bulk containers (IBCs) which were returnable. So, our part of the process was quite simple – we make the product in bulk, we ship it to him and then we support him in how he supplies customers.

It worked really well, Hamish delivered the products to all the different shops in London with his electric vehicles, then refilled any empty dispensers. It was the most efficient way of doing it, because he was only ever storing bulk products that he needed and everything was being refilled and reused, which is how we closed the loop.

It was really great having that process, where everything was just so direct.

We now also supply hundreds of stores around the UK so from that starting point the business has grown very organically. I would like to note that we don't actively go out and sell to people. Instead, it's been more organic and we've been approached first in most cases, so it's enabled the business to grow slowly, organically and give us time to iron out any kinks that come up.

We also buy 200 litre containers second-hand, then fix them up and fill them with our products. After that, we have a driver that delivers them to stores and fills a couple of bottles for them. Following that, when they're running low they can just place another order, and we'll take the old ones out and refill them.

When we started out, we couldn't believe that some places were prepared to commit to the volume of our products. I think though, because it comes straight from a factory it was really visual and they understood that we'd cut out all the packaging and the nonsense of storing, warehouses, logistics, etc.

We just made the products that went straight from the factory, to the van and then to the shop. People wanted to have it in their shops, and the loops were quite easy to close in most cases (apart from when some businesses were more than 100 miles away from us – but we worked it all out!).

We often plan our routes really carefully because of distance – and now of course we've moved towards a doorstep delivery.

The idea of the milkman has always been like a sort of romantic idea for me. I used to collect coke bottles when I was a kid and I thought they were really cool. I loved the idea that they were printed and they could be used again.

So from there we closed our loop with the electric fleet and we've had space to develop and grow as a company. So what was our idea?

Well, we've now invested in a bottle, washer and container so we have a lot more appeal to consumers visually and because of that we supply bagging boxes as well to people who order online.

We've perfected the bag and the box to a level where people can return an empty bag to us and we will refill it with products. From that though, it's our life's work to keep getting to a point where it's still sustainable and we have the best solution in terms of refills.

Something I will say about our journey as well, is just how important partnerships have been. They are so crucial in businesses, you should talk to other people and become inspired by them. We've really quizzed our suppliers,, although as much advice as we've taken on board we've ignored plenty as well.

Like we were told that we couldn't refill a bag, and a box bag but we did and we proved that it's something that's sustainable. We were also told that nobody would like the printed bottles that we use and people wouldn't reuse them. After all, you can buy drinks that are screen printed, but people throw them away. What would make people keep a bottle for cleaning products? But, our customers do keep them.

We also have a brilliant team and all these ideas have come from loads of different people. I'm a person that always has lots of ideas, so it's been important to me to create an atmosphere where people feel that they can come up with ideas and make suggestions. We're not frightened to get things wrong and try things out – which I think is really important for success.

An example of the above is we've been trying to find out how to use pallets. Some are carbon neutral, we tried oxygen biodegradable ones, then carbon nets but we weren't satisfied with any of them. Now, we've been trying to use them branded with paper – but we're working with our customers and looking into what they want and what we want. We want to be supplying something that is 100% plastic free in a closed loop product that people can use at home.

With investments and funding, we never raised anything. I was in a fortunate position that when we launched we had a business that worked parallel to us doing the same thing. So, our business has grown slowly over time because of that and as we couldn't throw money at it. Instead, it's just been a slow and long process. Everyone has had faith in us, but the biggest investment has been the people.

I think people are the best thing to invest in for your company. I couldn't ask for a better team and they look after the product on a day-to-day basis. In my eyes, it's so important in any business to find people that are better than you at doing things. I know what my limited skills are and what I'm able to do, so I've built a team that can make things happen.

However, I think the lab is very important because if you don't make the products that you say you're making, you don't have the ability to adapt and change. From that, you can't respond to all the feedback that you will get.

The biggest single investment we've had to make as a business though is definitely the bottle washer. It was a really important statement to make in a way; because as a small business we could achieve this method of suppliers. Yet, there are much bigger ones that cannot.

In terms of what's next, we launched haircare products in March, which is both exciting and terrifying. We don't send our products for consumer focus group testing; instead we make a product, we test it loads and all use it. Obviously we sent off for a third party testing as well and conduct all the cosmetic safety reports to ensure that it can be used. Yet, as we all use it you take it personally with how people react. After so much time making something you're bound to become attached.

Down the line, I've also got more projects and collaborations. I often seek people out that I want to work with and I have been talking to some companies that have waste streams and we would like to attempt to make products from their waste in the future. However, there's a big gulf between the idea and the reality.

CHAPTER ELEVEN

SARA AND ALICE - FRESH

WEBSITE: fresh.com/uk

Sarah and Alice have made FRESH, an all-inclusive wellbeing brand that launched recently. It focuses on fitness, dance, wellbeing, mental and physical health. They launched this during lockdown and as things reopen have expanded it further.

We originally planned to launch before lockdown, but didn't in time, so instead the time has allowed us to get our studio ready. We'd have days where both of us were doing classes in the morning, then meeting builders, then meeting a contractor, then more classes. The days would be very busy and pass quickly and we'd even end up painting in the evenings.

In terms of funding, we decided to look at a few different options for grants for sports. Sport England was one that stood out to us the most, as it was heavily focused on the community and that's one of our main goals. We wanted to support people in the community that may not necessarily be able to afford exercising or feel confident enough to enter a fitness facility.

So we both put together a pack of what our ethics were and how we wanted to run the business. Following that, we had to submit it to Sport England for approval and wait. It was quite a long process.

We had to jump through a lot of different hoops following the application, especially as COVID began. Sport England kept getting in touch with us and asking for more information, so we had to just keep following up. It was a lot of planning, guessing and estimating.

Thinking cost-wise was really important for us as well, so we broke everything down that we would spend the grant money on and they could see where their funding would go. In the end though, they did assign us a manager to walk us through all the steps which was really helpful.

When we were accepted for the grant, we started getting emails from them saying that they needed quotes on what we were planning and the work we wanted to do. They said they wanted to make sure we were being sensible with the money but as we had planned it all out we sent everything across.

Then the UK went into Lockdown in March.

Instead of opening the studio we launched an online brand at the same time as we were building our space up.

We both work well together and it's so important that you have that dynamic. Sometimes you need someone else to help you build something much bigger as starting out on your own can be very hard.

As there's two of us, it's really good – we each have our own strengths and weaknesses, but we balance each other out, so working together has been great.

Having someone else to bounce ideas off and work on different things also helps your business in a lot of ways too. I think it's really helped our business to grow and develop. We had days where there was a lot of self-doubt and the project seemed huge but having someone else there helps put things into perspective.

When the grant hit our account though, it wasn't until after we had started doing and purchasing things for the business. With Sport England, they give you the grant after you have ordered things, so we had to pay for everything upfront.

Our space needed a lot of work, and so we paid our builders first. The landlord of the space that we were renting from was very understanding though and gave us a three month rent free period. So, we did as much work as possible in that time before we began earning anything from the business.

In the end, the building work took up about 50% of our time. There was the air conditioning that needed to be redone and the sprung floor that we needed to get fitted (and it was an old gym floor that had condensation issues, so we had to take it up and replace it).

Although the grant was helpful in helping us to get established, we had to self-fund a number of different bits and pieces. For the lease for example our landlord was reluctant to take us on and we had to get guarantors for it all. In the end, we negotiated that we would put some money aside so if we ever did go bust, then he would be covered for the cost of having to find a new tenant.

So, we both ended up putting all of our savings on the line, into a joint bank account and prayed that we would get it all back.

It was definitely the right decision, and we keep all the interest that's accumulated – we actually made a profit on combining our funds ironically with the interest it built.

In the end, it was about £2,500 for the builders. It was all so new and it felt like so much money for us to invest into it, with absolutely no idea what the outcome would be.

When starting out, there were just so many things we didn't even think about in our physical space. Like a mould report, we didn't even know that one of those existed and then we ended up having to pay for one of those to get done.

We've had a few classes and have started running an in-house timetable for when the pandemic ends. We think that things will change though as people go back to a sense of normality. Through lockdown, we've been running virtual classes which were quite good but we are excited to have people in the studio.

The online platform has been doing really well and we're hoping to have something for everyone. I think this year in particular has put people into very different columns on how they feel about things, so it's important that we can meet those needs for people.

Now that restrictions are easing again, in the future we really want to get some workshops and seminars in. So it's not just a centre for people to come and hang out and get fit, but it actually provides a lot of services and skills that people can learn as well.

If we could give any advice to people who are going after grants – we would say to ask for more money. When we put the application together, we were trying to do it quickly and didn't get quotes. Taking the time to get quotes from various different places would've been a lot easier for us both.

The old saying is so true, in that you need to spend money to make money. You can only go so far without investments, so we would say to anyone to really get those funds if you can.

Another thing is that you should definitely consider being a social enterprise rather than a limited company, because there's a lot more availability for social enterprises or non-profit organisations.

CHAPTER TWELVE:

DAVID WARD - THE NURTURING CO.

WEBSITE: nurturing.life

The Nurturing Co is a sustainable home brand that creates, manufactures, and sells earth-friendly and modern brands. David Ward is the founder of this brand, and talks about how he started his journey to become an entrepreneur by chance!

I moved to Asia about seven years ago and at the time I was working in brand licensing in the fashion industry. During my time working in Asia, I was going through Japan on my way to China and I bumped into someone who was going the opposite way.

We met at a bar in Harajuku, Tokyo and started talking for a while. We spoke about everything from putting the world to rights and then eventually the topic of business came up.

I talked about what I did and the man I was talking with mentioned that he had an environmental cleaning company in Canada, Vancouver. Him and his parents were just about to launch a new product selection, which was bamboo and sugarcane toilet paper.

Due to the job I had at the time, I mentioned that I could probably help him find some partners for his brand and help with distribution in Asia.

After that night, we went our separate ways but kept in touch so I could help him with the distribution and finding partners.

I went away from that meeting being very fascinated – it was my first ever introduction to the idea that you could make toilet paper from something other than wood pulp (the brand is also called Caboo, which is currently doing very well in both Canada and the US!).

When I went back to Singapore I started doing all the market research to help with their product launches. However, I found that there wasn't anything I could use, not to mention there were some very big differences for the consumer requirements when it came to the final product.

So, from that we needed to fill these big gaps in terms of research which he couldn't do at the time. I said that I would create another brand as a solution to get around this in terms of the consumer requirements, market research, etc.

That way, we would have two brands and it would be more interesting and there was more that we could do with it. In the end, it didn't work out like we hoped and we just ended up staying with our own brand.

There were many complications, like making new packaging, new branding, the language differences, and other things of that nature. So, in the end that became the first sustainable homecare product that was available in Southeast Asia called No Trees. It's still available in Singapore and you can also buy it in the US.

Although it was such a big thing for me at the time, I was going against the grain in a lot of ways, I didn't really know anybody who was doing anything like this. Seven years ago, nobody was having conversations about sustainable products and businesses – so it very much felt like I was on my own.

In fact, most people weren't registering that there might be a problem down the line. So it was very, very difficult to get people interested in this brand and what we were doing. Luckily for us, a wealthy family became interested in what we were doing and from there I managed to sell the idea then I created a business and job for myself in the process.

From that, over the next two and a half years, with the man I had met by chance, we created this brand and built up a healthy, sustainable business. We launched it in Singapore and then eventually the US, but through it all, I just kept asking myself what we could do better.

Through this journey with the brand, I kept learning more – so even though I was focused on sustainable toilet paper, I found out new things. For example, 45% - 65% of wipes are made from plastic.

I realised that we needed to become more dynamic and really look at what we were doing to be different from other brands – but a lot of people didn't really want to make the change to having something different.

When it came down to it – I knew that I had to walk away from the career I had already made for myself and start all over again. Which is never an easy thing to do.

I needed to understand the purpose of what I was doing with the toilet paper and why I had created the brand in the first place. In the end, it felt like a simple decision and I resigned from the fashion industry.

I had been in the fashion industry for over 25 years at this point, but just moved completely away from it into sustainable products. I had a great life in the fashion industry – I travelled, met wonderful people, inspiring leaders, but it wasn't what I truly felt like I was meant to do.

There was this yearning inside of me, telling me that I needed to do something about this problem and I knew that I just had to leap into it feet first. So, I was back to square one – I had a completely blank slate to work on.

I actually sat down, and wrote on a piece of paper to help navigate what I wanted, and wrote one sentence across the top of it – which said no single-use plastics. So, that became the goal of the next six-eight months. I contacted various different suppliers that I had already worked with to become known and to know whether it was feasible for me to do. Also, would they do it?

To my surprise, a lot of them bit the bullet and helped us create versions of the things they produced for other companies, but without any of the plastics. That was probably the first major hurdle that we had.

After we had tackled that challenge, we began identifying suppliers who were doing the best they could in creating a product that was sustainable and could be managed in terms of a long-term business both for them and the people they were working with.

Bamboo, unlike other resources used by corporations, is grown by individual farmer families who own a piece of land. They chop down their bamboo by hand, then they get given the market rate for it, which sustains their family as a small, independent business that can grow into something else – so we started the company with that in mind and that we were going to try and do one better.

We found that we could drastically reduce the amount of plastic and offer an alternative model to a lot of things. We ended up making refillable versions of products that had more than a single use and continued to look at what products existed and tried to figure out what we could do for both the consumer and the earth.

Then, we moved onto crowdfunding, though this was a more secondary marketing campaign – especially after COVID happened.

COVID last year did two things to our business – it totally wiped out our toilet paper stock. The craziness of bulk buying that happened as a result of the lockdown meant that we went completely out of stock! Then lots of people thought – well how am I going to go to the toilet if the toilet paper has been sold out everywhere?

So, the bidet market found themselves inundated with people that were prepared to make the shift across – which I thought was great. Every day for four years on a morning when I went to the toilet the first thing that would come into mind is that we have to figure out a better way to do this.

Even with bamboo, it is a truly sustainable and regenerative plant. Yet, it's still something that you use once.

I eventually got the bidet in my home and loved it, but it took a good six months or so to convince my wife to use it on a regular basis. Then, every time I would speak to companies that were doing bidets predominately it was never the right time for them to introduce it to Asia.

So, in April I just thought well I'm not going to wait anymore – COVID meant that companies were running out of toilet paper and the market for bidets was far better. Within three or four days, we had the brand name, then we got to work on the packaging and suppliers, and tried to get rid of any plastic that could be used.

We eliminated the plastics that could've been used in the packaging – so there's no plastic bags or anything. We also made sure that it was a very simple and easy to adjust to, and that it could fit whatever people needed.

It takes just 20 minutes to fit, and not to mention, it's saving you money because you've got the price of the bidet vs what you would use buying toilet rolls. On average, after seven months you reap the financial rewards. But for an environmentally driven company, the statistics that showed why people should shift to it were quite compelling.

I've been in this space for over 10 years now and we still only have about 6% of the global hygiene market. The big guys hold the big guns, they've got millions of dollars and they're not going to give up their brand that easily. They've done a very good job of persuading us for a long, long time that there is no better alternative than your favourite brand, the brand that you love, etc.

Except, there are better alternatives – of course there is! They're deliberately hiding dirty secrets from us – like the fact that 27,000 trees get cut down just to make toilet paper and then recycled paper requires at least 45% - 65% of virgin fibre.

The above is called overproduction of virgin recycled materials. It basically means that more trees are getting cut down each day just to make more paper. Sadly, it uses an enormous amount of water to make a whole roll, in fact it takes 37 gallons of water to make one roll of wood pulp toilet paper.

Nowadays, consumers are only just beginning to hear from both the government and from other leading bodies on what your carbon footprint is. The realisation that everything has a carbon impact is sort of dawning on all of us, and wood pulp tissue paper needs at least two grams of carbon per sheet of toilet paper.

So, to give you an example of that, if every home in Singapore used our toilet rolls for one year, it would stop 72 million grams of carbon being used. So, that's why we launched the bidet, we're not moving enough people over to bamboo. Regardless of what brand it is, whether it's ours or anyone else's, we're not making these changes fast enough to stop the destruction of forests around the world.

Crowdfunding for our project was messy as well – my advice to any self-startups would be not to set your objectives too high. For us, we had a brand that nobody really knew about, so it didn't really make it on a lot of people's radar.

We learnt a lot though from the process of doing it, like looking at what your goal was and where other people were at from it. Like some places get millions of dollars for certain things and then others, just bite the dust.

I think our problem was that we didn't focus a lot of attention on the pre-launch phase, which gets you a lot of traction. I think another thing is that how do you market something that isn't readily available to people? That they can't access until the crowdfunding project has finished?

Then eventually that traction goes away – people who pledged to us, they send us emails asking am I still going to get one, even if you don't make it? And of course we can't tell them, because we can't say more on it until the crowdfunding has ended.

There we definitely shot ourselves in the foot a little by setting our objectives higher, because we didn't need to do that.

It was a great process for us to go through all the same – it disciplined you to prepare your communication more, your product and brands story, to understand the process of how you might want to communicate the benefits of your product, how to include the other people in your sphere. It was a great process for us to go through because it pushed us to think hard about the pricing of the product and how we might communicate it.

From that we actually ended up making a funny video, which we probably wouldn't have done otherwise. Crowdfunding just really pushed us outside of our comfort zone and it helped me look at the bigger picture.

My main focus had always been just getting a great product, but that really helped to expand it.

The moment where we got the product – when it arrived in the warehouse was probably the best moment though. We had pre sold them and then having them shipped out, and when people installed them and said how much they loved them, it was there that I felt really accomplished with it all.

Now that we are launching' in the UK, we've had a different approach after our experience. We have been in direct communication with individual investors, who've questioned us on our brand, our segments and such.

It's been difficult in some ways as well, as to begin with the investors don't know anything about you at that stage. There's also been the matter of pricing issues because of the freight movement with China.

The cost of shipping between China and the UK has increased by over 350% and in particular it went up over the Chinese New Year. So, that's been a real problem for us and we've not really found an answer to that, only that shipping is gradually coming back down.

From that, we are hoping to move products in the UK in April – although initially we were hoping to move them straight away. Yet, because of the above shipping pricing has just become extortionate.

Something that would've cost you $4,000 suddenly became over up to 14x the cost even though it wasn't a particularly big item. Then, Brexit happened of course which made it even more complicated – especially for shipping goods.

Then, the last biggest hurdle was getting a bank account. COVID created all kinds of problems, but in terms of opening a UK business accounts that was the hardest. We were a foreign entity so to speak, and getting that door open took a lot of work, conversations and so much more.

All in all though, I'm really glad that we've given people better options that are more environmentally friendly.

CHAPTER THIRTEEN

ELIZA FLANAGAN - KANKAN

WEBSITE: kankan.london

KanKan is an innovative and alternative brand that does away with single use plastic soap bottles. It is cruelty free and uses natural ingredients for their hand wash, body wash and other products. Their packaged products are in cans that are better for the environment and for their consumers.

I'm Eliza and my Cofounder is Mary. We were both friends and then decided one day to build a business that had a really important mission.

A mission statement is so important – it literally defines your brand. We both wanted to do something that was sustainable as we learned that single use plastics in the bathroom are rarely recycled and that became our mission – to reduce that.

Plastics themselves are horrible for the environment, every year about 8 million tons of plastic waste goes into the ocean and most of them can take up to 400 years to break down.

Those are horrifying facts and that was the start of what we wanted to change. We wanted to produce a product that could get to the market quickly, so we didn't want to be too innovative in packaging.

We needed something that wouldn't cost a great deal of money and when digging deeper, we learned that any kind of new material in the world of waste can be more dangerous or hazardous than one that's pre-existing. This is because there's no waste streams that are set up to support them.

So, Mary and I pivoted and we said to ourselves, we'll need to use material that is really valuable and aluminium was one that we decided upon.

It's not perfect, no packaging really is – but it is infinitely recyclable which is obviously a brilliant thing. It has almost global waste streams that are established and commonplace. Then, it's also the only material of its kind that pays for its own collection and helps pay for other waste stream collections as well, so there's a lot of positives about the material.

We also needed a material that could easily carry liquids, that was both secure and light and aluminium fitted perfectly. It was such a humble element, which seems unambiguous but has such a classic design.

They're incredibly light and robust and there's huge amounts of systems globally that use them. So, you know you've got vending machines that use them and you see them every day in the supermarkets. In a way, it was mad that it was only used for beverages, they're so commonplace.

To us, it just seemed so wacky that nobody else had done this, it was crazy. There are a few people that are using them now, but I think we were the first of its kind.

So when we set it up, we tested the market using a minimum viable product (MVP), which is an early version of a product given to customers who then provide feedback for future products you make. We've done that over the course of the last year and self-funded the business, then we just put it out into the market.

We focused really heavily on the branding, to make sure it had this elevated brand so it had a very premium look and feel, just to see if people would buy something that was very elegant. We really wanted to see if people would engage with it – and they did.

People don't use cans for everything still though, and we've learned a lot when deciding to use the material. There was a woman who deals in cans and Mary spoke to her about the different ones we could use. In the end we realised that they are incredibly complicated. They are fickle, fragile and quite difficult to mould into what you want, especially when you're using them in a non-fizzy or gassy product, because they are made of aluminium which is a soft material in itself.

Aluminium can bend and even though they don't split open or anything they do mark very easily as well. We're trying to improve this as we go along, but it is a design that we're very proud of.

We've also recently launched a new design for the cans, which has a 360° lid which you can pull open. Originally this design was actually intended for just craft beers, so when you open the whole lid you can drink directly from the can. The theory behind it was that you get more of the aroma of the beer if the can opening was larger, so when we first saw the can we thought to ourselves well we can really use this for soap, because it's much more accessible.

So we ended up going for that design, the lid gives you more flexibility and it does help you pour the soap into your containers, making refills far easier.

With making the soap, we wanted to make sure it was sustainable in that regard as well. We didn't want to get any of our products manufactured outside of England, because we're only selling to the UK at the moment.

We wanted to make sure that we could reduce the amount of transport we use, and from that we managed to find a manufacturer down in Devon. They manufacture natural products and there were a lot of things about them that really resonated with our brand, we wanted a product that was really high-quality for us, and we were really happy to find that.

With the soap, we weren't the makers and wanted to leave it to the professionals. I think when you're doing something on a kind of industrial scale as well, you need to make sure your focus is in the right places. We wanted this brand to be really big and have a high impact, and if we were making everything ourselves, we wouldn't be able to do that sort of thing as our attention was elsewhere.

Sustainability is of course very important, but there's so many problems with it. Big brands like Ben & Jerry's for example mention it, but they aren't doing enough. You need to be honest and upfront in what exactly you're doing to be sustainable and that kind of honesty attracts customers so much more.

Customers in particular are starting to ask the harder questions as well like what does sustainability mean to you? What does ethical mean? What efforts are you making that proves to us that you're being sustainable? Can you show us the thinking and the methods behind it?

I think it makes it harder, because you want to be as clear cut as you can, but also not bombard them with all the facts. It can be overwhelming when you look into everything, because there's so much around it all.

We actually set up Sustainable Development Goals with a Sustainability Consultant. They helped us right from the beginning on what to do but at the same time it was so overwhelming looking at all the different options. In the end, we picked out three or four which resonated with our brand and values and focused on those.

With any business you want to be sustainable, but you also want to do everything and tick every box but it's almost impossible. To do that and be financially viable as a business is so hard, especially if you're a small start-up company because everything is so expensive and costly.

With our next steps, we're starting to fundraise – as we've been completely self-funded up until this point. We have loads of things we want to do and launch with a bunch of new products. We've decided that we're going to dip into haircare and do things like moisturisers and bath oils, but we need to make sure we can finance it.

The thing I'm most excited about though is our dispenser – we're looking at one where you put the can inside the dispenser and it pumps directly from it. At the moment, people have been emptying the soap into their reusable bottles, which is not bad, but we want to add a bit more user experience that's smoother.

To fundraise we're doing a Crowdcube so we're trying to get partners on board. It's a huge bit of work, but the brand itself is fairly simple so we're hoping that people can catch onto it.

Overall, it can be a lot of work getting funding but we eventually found an interesting business called Ice Q. They are basically hand-holders through the process of fundraising and it's very enjoyable as they tell you step-by-step on what to do.

It was really good for us having that guidance to get through it all. Crowdfunding in particular teaches people so much about their business and the details of it.

I think the key take away that people should have from this though is how important your mission statement and brand is – we wanted something sustainable that people could use and were really passionate about delivering that.

Chapter Fourteen:
Tom Meades - Gomi Design

WEBSITE: Gomi.design

Gomi design is a company that transforms waste materials into popular technological products. Their items are produced from various different waste materials, like recycled plastic bags and repurposed batteries to create innovative products.

Gomi Design basically started as a way to reuse materials that aren't currently being reused. During my final year of university I was doing a sustainable design materials course and it was all about testing and playing with new materials to see what we could make.

I learned then that plastic bags couldn't actually be recycled at that time – in 2017. So, councils were just not taking them and people had no idea how to dispose of them in a better way.

One million plastic bags end up in the trash every minute, and the world uses over 50 billion a year. They have such a harmful impact on the world around us, but originally I was just fascinated that they weren't able to be recycled.

Then I discovered that I could make a really beautiful marbled material from the waste of plastic bags and that's where it all started.

I wanted to explore making tech products as well, as they're a very untapped market and they are the least sustainable products of them all and then it just grew into what it is today.

We started out the product using Kickstarter, which is a really cool platform for start-ups, so we've used it as a way to work out how much interest there is in a product before we make a huge batch.

Last year, we reached the portable chargers on Kickstarter and it was our first more affordable product that we've made. It was powered by e-bike batteries that were reclaimed – the first in the world to do so.

At the time we said; "Let's make a product that's affordable but also sustainable, but do we know if people want it?"

So, we put it on Kickstarter and raised over £30,000 in crowdfunding which was incredible! It showed us that people were really interested in these products and that's how it all started really.

After that, we spent a couple of months making the products. Kickstarter works with pre-orders so you know how many you've got to make. Then, we put the product on the website so we can start selling it.

It's actually quite funny in a way, as we launched it in the first week of lockdown.

We were going to hold off the launch at first, because we were like well it's a portable charger, people aren't going to take this around the house because of lockdown. At the same time though, we had put all this work into it so decided to just launch it and it was very successful.

Then, this year we've just launched a new product for our speakers and we're following that same ethos. So, is there really an interest in the product? We've made it affordable and collaborated with Lime.

Lime has e-bikes in London, so we've taken 50,000 shells from their old bikes and used it to power a new range of speakers. It was a really cool project – and it was perfect for Kickstarter as we got to tell this story.

Like before, when putting it on Kickstarter we could see how much interest we got in the products so we didn't have to guess and order the other components for the speakers in the thousands. The speaker is doing really well, after our first weekend launching it on there, we already hit £30,000.

In terms of finding people to collaborate with, we've been quite lucky in a lot of ways – especially with PR and getting featured in different places. As a start-up especially, you're competing with all these big companies so you need to try and be out there as much as possible and push the boundaries of the products you're making so that it will be featured in as many places as possible.

Nobody else was using repurposed batteries or plastic bags, so we had the upper hand and we just thought; "let's do it, let's try and make this work."

I think in particular, being brave in the materials and products you're making pays off in terms of the features you get. Brands are more aware of you, they're more likely to collaborate with you because they've seen you get featured. They want their brand to do more good things because it's good for them and good for the planet.

In terms of marketing it's also a really good thing for brands to show. People are changing their mindsets a lot, and they want brands to be held more accountable for the waste they produce, so being associated with us has a really good impact for them.

For us though, we're just trying to be as out-there as possible with what we're making. We want to get the features, then reach out and get the collaborations as well.

The collaborations themselves aren't as glamorous as people may think though, it's mainly just me messaging hundreds of people and then getting one reply back that works out. So, I think you just have to be relentless and keep going, messaging as many people as you can and really get people interested in what you're doing.

We mostly use Instagram for promoting products, but LinkedIn is also very useful for reaching out to people. It's not spam either when you're trying to message all these people. It's like you're actually trying to do something good for the planet and a lot of these companies want to do good things.

Showing interest in the people you want to collaborate with is so important as well, you have to make sure that when you contact them you make a really good impression.

Kickstarter - where it all started - was funny in a way as well, we reached a huge customer base, but to begin with we were selling the product at a discount. You don't really make much profit from it at all and for us any money went into buying the stock, making it and making the chargers.

For us, Kickstarter was never about making profit – instead it was more about gauging interest in our products. It literally just funds the production and a bit extra, like working on a new process but that's it really.

Now, our main goal is to try and industrialise the process a bit more. So at the moment we're working with maybe 30-40 kilos of plastic a day. With the new process that we're working on we're going to be able to use over 500 kilos.

We're just really trying to innovate that area and the more interest we have, the closer we are to getting to that.

If someone was looking to do a crowdfunding campaign for their product, I would say that it's more work than a full-time job. It's felt like a 100-hour week job putting it together but it's so good for your brand to get it out there.

I do want to just say though, I don't think it's for everyone. You've really got to analyse whether it's right for your brand or not. If you do end up going ahead with it, the main thing is to reach out and tell as many people as you can about it.

With start-ups, you don't have the advertising funds, so just reaching out to people like your family, your friends, your friends of friends and asking them to share what you're doing is so important. You just need to try and get it out everywhere.

You also need to make sure the cost of products is low on Kickstarter as well because people are investing in a brand that they don't necessarily trust. It's a brand that's new in the market and although they want to support you and help, it's a risk that they need to take and if it's too expensive they may think well, I'm not sure I trust them that much.

With start-ups as well, you don't have the graphic design, the branding or anything else that makes it looks super slick and appealing. So the kick-starters that are really successful from start-ups are usually products that are between £20 - £40.

Talking to people is where you gain the most traction though. We even reached out to the Kickstarter team when we set it up – as we're definitely not experts – and asked all kinds of questions like have you got any advice? They're really helpful as well and it's good for their platform when people succeed.

Being open, humble and admitting that things might not be successful really helps you to keep going. You just try your best and do everything you can to make it work.

This speaker that we've launched recently isn't actually our first, we tried launching one about three years ago and it was our first. We did everything wrong. Every single possible thing that you could do wrong, we did. It was fine at the end though, it was a learning curve even if we didn't get the funding.

We set our target at £40,000 which we thought was great, whereas nobody does that, because if it doesn't reach near the target nobody is going to back it. They're not going to want to put funds into something that's not going to achieve its goal and lose out on getting products.

So, we learned from that and we were lucky enough that the exposure we got from Kickstarter, even though it didn't pay off, we did get orders. People were still ordering from us.

We actually got an order from Heineken where there was a house party in Berlin, and they had loads of waste from the party but they wanted to make speakers for the people who went to it. It was really amazing having them reach out to us to make these.

They sent us the waste from the party, and we made the speakers and sent them out. It was really cool. Kickstarter gets you PR that you wouldn't get from just putting it on your website, so even if it doesn't work out how you expect there's still pros from it.

For future products, last year we released a portable charger, this year we've released wireless chargers and speakers, so now we're looking at possibly releasing another product in the summer.

For collaborations, we've had a lot of good ones, we did the trophies for the British Independent film Awards, like these crazy prismic sort of structures. Working on collaborations with brands is always really fun, so we've had a lot of different and interesting products.

A lot of people tend to think that if you have an idea and just launch it then suddenly everyone will be climbing all over you but that's not how it all works. We had to put in so much work, like the design of the page, how we laid things out, reaching out to people – you just need to try and get as much traction as you can.

If you try and charge a really high-end price for something as well, you're going to really struggle, especially with Kickstarter. People need to be ready for the possible fallout of that.

We had a videographer take good photos and videos of our products and I was quite lucky, as I lived in Brighton and had a lot of creative friends. From that, I didn't really have to spend loads of money on content. From that, it's worked out really nicely for us but then as we've grown bigger we've had to put more funding into it.

Research is also so important – if you're starting out make sure you look at what other people are doing. Especially on Kickstarter, what are they doing? How are they gaining traction? That kind of thing.

CHAPTER FIFTEEN:
JOSIE MORRIS - WOOLCOOL

WEBSITE: woolcool.com

Woolcool is a sustainable packaging brand that has changed the way food stuffs and pharmaceuticals are shipped. They are kept at a constant temperature and are founded on sustainability to protect the contents of their shipments and the planet.

My mother actually invented Woolcool in the early 2000s, she was a Packaging Designer and Consultant. One of her clients was the National Trust, and they called upon her expertise to develop a way to send their tenant farmer's meat through mail order, direct to the consumer, without using polystyrene. At the time, it was the only material that was used to send chilled produce.

After being given the remit, she then went away and tested some different materials and came across wool as a fantastic insulator. In the end it outperformed polystyrene and she sold a batch into the National Trust. Then the rest is history.

She went back to her day job, but ended up getting recommended and contacted by a few different people wanting Woolcool. So in 2008 she decided to set up Woolcool officially as she saw the need for a sustainable solution for the shipment of both medicine and food.

To begin with it was mostly supplied for use with food products but it expanded quickly into the Pharmaceutical sector. Wool is a really awesome insulator and – although I'm biased – scientifically it has been proven. Basically because of how wool has evolved over 1000s of years, their fibres have developed to trap air within the fibre, creating a thermal barrier. It's been used for thousands of years because of its many fantastic properties.

As we expanded, we wanted to use it in a place where it's performance would be really important. We wanted to do something that could help save lives. Temperature control is so important in transportation with medicine.

You may have seen the news about the COVID vaccines for example, they have very set temperatures that they need to remain at and the insulation of our packages does just that.

Even before COVID, we were supplying into the pharmaceutical sector and a lot of the development of our products are focused on that. Food is also a big part of what we do, it's very important that food is shipped safely and sustainably.

Packaging is so important in the shipment of goods, keeping them safe, secure and intact. Although there are plenty of cheap solutions on the market, companies are looking for more sustainable options and those that approach us see the value in what we offer. On top of that many use Woolcool as a marketing opportunity, they can say they're doing their part for the environment.

There's benefits to using any solution, our materials means that you use less material, fewer ice packs and it's natural, compostable, reusable and renewable.

When we first started, we self-funded it and were independent. There was a little bit of investment from the outside very early on, which was paid back, so we remain independent and completely privately family owned.

We also did qualify for grants and government funding. Between 2011 and 2015 we received government funding for a project based on pharmaceutical development six We used this to research, develop and really delve into all the science behind the wool and its performance.

Grants are often something that people don't really look into for businesses as they take time, but I think that they definitely should. Although that being said, some grants are linked to how many jobs you can create and then that creates more capital expenses. So for example if we bought a machine, we create five jobs and you get a 30% grant.

Then if you're doing something that is innovative and could be seen as viable in the UK, you're more likely to get a bigger grant. I think that the challenge of it all is that what you're creating may not go where you want to go, but that's fine, it may be that you open up a new market!

I must say though, in terms of the grants we had, they were very supportive. You have to fill out the forms, make sure that you're eligible and make sure it's right for you. I'm not necessarily an advocate of consultants for everything, but I think that they certainly have their value with this kind of thing. We had an amazing guy that helped us with all of that.

Finding investments is a really good way to use consultants, and these things can honestly be so time consuming for you when you have a business or you don't have the knowledge to do it yourself. These things take time, and they take away time from you working on the business which is obviously the number one goal.

We also got our B Corp status recently, and whilst I've been aware of it for a while I just never really felt like we were in the right position to do it or it was the right time.

The process actually started in September – October 2019 and we became certified in February 2020. In a way it sets you apart from those that are claiming to do something to those who are actually doing it. The network it gives you and the support to keep improving is just incredible as well.

The decision to apply was quite easy in the end, we just decided to bite the bullet and go for it. So I worked with the team to gather the information needed, although looking back if I did it again, I probably would have looked for support from someone outside of the organisation. In the end, I just went off and thought we're just going to do this.

It was actually a very big project, but I think it's good that it took so long to assess and for them to award it, because it shows they're really dedicated to awarding it to the right brands.

The B Corp status also opens you up to groups of people to connect with. Businesses are often viewed as monsters – they just eat everything up and because of that a lot are seen very negatively. I think the reality though is every business is like a person, and has a different personality and many are just trying to do the best they can.

Most businesses are trying to do the right things and make changes, that are fighting to make things change socially and environmentally. But the difficulty lies in knowing how to do it.

Then that's where the B Corp comes in, they ask you things like: How can you sustain this long term? How can you reduce your carbon footprint? Where do you start with it all? How do you reduce your energy usage? How do you make incentives for your staff in a way that's fair and right, making them feel engaged?

There's so many questions they ask, but as a business as a whole, it needs to have the heart to want to make those changes and be able to answer those questions. The network and the community around B Corp is definitely something that helps you to improve and encourage that.

Going forward we're looking more at sustainable growth as a business so that we can continue to do the right thing and invest in our people.

People and the planet are very intrinsically linked – if you look after your people, you look after the planet, and then there is this triangle of looking after each other.

I don't want to say we're sustainable just for the environment as well, I want us to be sustainable as a business. We're not necessarily going for high growth trajectory with highs and lows, investors, grant funding, etc. We just want to try and be a business with a positive, strong legacy rather than targeting the quickest growth we can before disappearing or floating.

If you are starting out though I would say marketing is key. You don't have to spend loads, but making sure you've got a good brand from the start is key – if you've got a good brand, you've got a good reputation that sets you apart from your competitors.

Having the right people around you is so important as well, and I think that's why we've managed to get to the place we have. I believe in making sure people feel engaged, feel involved and enjoy being at work. Investing in your people is so important, because you get so much more back than what you invested, and they get personal development and satisfaction – so believe in it and follow your gut.

CHAPTER SIXTEEN:
HARRY NORRIS - BIG LITTLE BRANDS

WEBSITE: biglittlebrands.co.uk

Big little brands is a company that is a platform that makes eco-conscious shopping possible. They make sure all their products are sourced ethically and eco-consciously. They also donate some of their profits to charity to help fund various projects all over the world.

I was in my second year of university and it was then that I decided to try and set up a small business of my own. It started as an active wear company and it wasn't particularly successful.

It sort-of started, but I didn't really know how much time and attention it needed. It got in the way of my university work and eventually it just sort of shut itself down. It wasn't really what I wanted, but then I noticed that there was this huge community of students that all had small businesses – and they were doing sustainable things.

There were just all these great businesses with great products that were sustainable but they weren't getting the recognition that they deserved.

I think that it's a problem for so many businesses, they have such strong products but they don't really get the audience that they deserve with it all. So, having done my small business and seeing it fail, then having all these ideas around me I decided to start Big Little Brands.

It's basically like an online marketplace, a bit like Amazon or Etsy and it has real people that make sustainable products. So, for me I became a part of that community and was able to go to all these businesses and say that I was going to put their products onto this one site.

It was really straightforward and it was the answer for where to buy from small businesses and shop sustainably.

We've now got lots of different businesses, some are bigger than others. We usually approach ones that are run by one or two people, that are locally made and locally sourced and we do a lot of our research on Instagram.

We can sort of gauge how big someone is from their Instagram content, although we are also wary that sometimes it can be completely wrong. So I think we just try and steer away from businesses that we know have a good reputation and are already quite established. Instead, we have our sights set on the smaller ones that are trying to become more established.

In the future, I would love to see one of our businesses blow up and become the next big thing – but it's something we'll have to look at in future. We want to maintain that small business approach.

Usually the businesses that you have are really local and have a personal touch to it as well. The person that packs the order is the owner, the person that sends you the email is the owner and if you have any issues it's the owner. Customer experience with those smaller brands are second to none, and I think that's really what we try and aim for and are in the sort of onboarding process.

We don't hold the stock or do anything for the businesses either. It's a lot like Depot – you create your own account and then you have a dashboard. I think in the future we'd like to hold stock, so that we can offer free delivery and things like that, or do promotions but with small businesses you just get the extra customised touch. You'll have a handwritten thank you note and some extra bits and pieces and it just adds something more to it.

I ordered a hoodie from one of our companies and they sent a packet of seeds with it to grow your own flowers. If we held stock that personal touch would be lost, because we could put the seeds in but you wouldn't get the same touch to it all.

Our entire goal is just about helping small businesses and that's how we get so many sales through the door. We want people to hear about these businesses and really understand how incredible these people are. These people often work two, three jobs and then they're doing this on the side. They put so much effort into how it's sourced, how it's made, how it's packaged and they deserve to be recognised.

With investors I was very, very lucky. My family really supported the idea and I was given a family loan from my parents to set up the website. From there, it's been a group project where we have our monthly running costs and those are funded by me on a month-to-month basis.

In the beginning I invested in people that were smarter than me. It wasn't anything to be scared of, I just had to find talented people that could really help me along with this.

I was quite lucky in another way, as I had two amazing friends that were very talented and came along to help me make the business. Then I hired a social media manager called Kate who came in and pushed the brand further.

She just helped our Instagram sky-rocket to a new level and now we've hired someone else who's just pushing it further and further. I know it's easier said than done that you just need to hire good people, I do understand how lucky I was to have friends who didn't charge me much and find a great social media manager off the bat. But, I think it's really important to have someone that you can bounce ideas off of, who argues against you when you have a point and that really pushes you. That in itself is invaluable and so if you can invest in someone like that, it will get you where you need to go.

From there I hired a few more people and the whole team just gels together really well. Everyone has the same goal and it's a great atmosphere.

Our brand is still quite young, we only launched our website in December, so we're always looking to take on new brands. The important thing about marketplaces is that we want to make sure that our consumers have as much choice as they can.

We're actually starting to invest in a new website as well, as at the beginning I was very naïve in business terms. I didn't really know how businesses worked and from that I made a lot of mistakes.

In particular, I made a lot of mistakes in trusting people that I should've looked into more – so when the website was built, I didn't really like how it looked, how it handled, or the user journey. This was something that I only realised recently though and that I've become more aware of as our journey progressed.

We're hoping that when we create this new website, it will really help people find what they're looking for, and in the next few months we just want to get our names out as much as we can.

We try to run a social media page that's engaging, we do videos that explain the things happening in terms of sustainability, we do interviews with our brands and now it's just about taking it to the next level when our business gets upgraded.

The vetting process for all these brands we have is very important as well, we can't just list every brand we come across as we're very careful on who we onboard. Our team is great and they know exactly where we want to be.

A term I often use is we want to be getting on people's plates which basically means, can we get in front of people? People don't really know about us yet, can we get our name out there?

And for us that's the most important thing for now.

CHAPTER SEVENTEEN:

TWO DRIFTERS DISTILLERY

WEBSITE: twodriftersrum.com

Two Drifters Distillery is a British-made and award winning rum. It's the first rum distillery of its kind to leave a negative carbon footprint. It's founded by Russ and Gemma Wakeham who love rum and the planet.

Two Drifters is actually born out of the time we spent in Vancouver. At the time, I was a Research Chemist and every two years, we got dragged all over the place. We would change jobs constantly searching for money to do our research.

Then we spent some time in Vancouver and I found it very inspiring. They have craft breweries on almost every block and you end up cycling between the breweries because it's so vibrant and everyone's doing different things.

When we came back to the UK, we wanted to start building something for ourselves. We got a place with a garage with somewhere that we could start brewing in, so we spent all of our evenings brewing beer and then after some time we just got better and better at doing it.

At first, we sold it right out of the garage after we got our licences sorted and all that stuff, but it got to a point so quickly where we just couldn't make enough. People loved it and we said to each other, right, now's the time that we need to quit our jobs and set up the brewery.

The plan was always to use the brewery to try and build a rum distillery and what we found was that we could get the equipment within our budget – a small scale version basically. So it started with a 2000 litre brewery and an 83 litre distillery. So, we sold our house to pay to do it and basically it was a huge contrast between the two.

Within three to six months we started selling and we quickly realised we couldn't make enough rum to keep up with demand. We rethought it all and switched to making rum on the beer equipment, so we converted it all.

The change was fast! We went from making about 80 bottles a week of rum to over 2000 bottles a week. So it was a big swing in what we did.

We always wanted to sell rum as well, our first date with my now-wife and I was rum tasting and then on our honeymoon we went to St Lucia because of rum. I wasn't into rum, I always kind of considered it like a cocktail spirit and then I was introduced to the sipping rum and it was amazing.

I often think there is a rum for everyone, and if you say you don't like it, then you just haven't tried the right one.. It's an amazing spirit, whether it's in a cocktail, with a mixer, on its own, with ice, without ice, in coffee – anything really. I just love the versatility of rum.

We often get asked if we'd ever make a gin, but rum is what we do best, so we are definitely a rum facility.

The real challenge of rum making was also the licences and all that stuff to get sorted. If you want to make gin for example, you can do it with a rectifier or compounding licence, which is basically where you buy the spirit ready-made.

It's like 95% alcohol and then you would flavour it with your own style and aroma. Rum is very different, we start with the raw ingredients and ferment it, then distil it. As the process is very different you need more licences, especially as you're working with things like methanol and solvents, you need to make sure it's all safe.

We're very different from the rum and gin distilleries that you see as well, as a lot of them tend to buy the alcohol ready-made and flavour it. We were never going to do that though, we always wanted to make it from the raw ingredients.

In terms of how we first financed it all, my wife was a freelance social media manager at the time. We had a young child, so she was at home a lot and helped to make the beer. Then, we got very good at making the beer and people wanted to buy it.

We needed to create a company name, and as Gemma had walked up the aisle to Moon River, we decided on Two Drifters (off to see the world).

Then our jobs were starting to come to their natural end as well, we weren't really enjoying work as much. Every night we'd come home and make beer, sell beer at the local fairs and things and it just felt like it was time to take a leap of faith.

There was a demand for us, so we just went with it and then we had to find ways to keep the business going. We decided to sell our house, move home to Devon, find a warehouse and start the process of setting up a brewery and distillery. In terms of the house we sold it and moved in with our parents. That allowed us to buy the equipment, lease the premises, get the licences sorted and start selling.

The biggest thing we've invested in though, that's made a real impact on our growth, has definitely been social media marketing. Gemma runs all the social media and it's really helped us hit the ground running. Marketing can be so expensive as well, but investing in digital marketing courses allows us to understand where to put our products, where to change the conversation in each field and that kind of thing.

Having that ability to be able to market yourself has been great for us as well, we've definitely saved a lot of costs throughout our time in building all this. Now, we're at a point where we're looking to outsource some bits and pieces as we've grown, but it's taken a while to get to a place where we're in a comfortable enough position to do that.

Now we're in a really good position and have been using crowdfunding to improve our packaging and designs. That's what the future is about, just improving our capacity, efficiency, bringing down costs, bringing in new packaging, new photos, new cocktails, everything that means we can shout our story louder and clearer .

My advice to anyone is make sure that you have an end goal firmly in your sights. I think that when you have in mind what your end goal is, it will be easier to know the direction you're travelling in and make decisions easier.

With crowdfunding as well, it's a lot of work and I think people often don't really think of it like that – but it was definitely a full time job for us. There's so much work in crowdfunding and you can't even go live with it without raising half the money. You need to convince people that you're a great investment, and you are being scrutinised very heavily.

It was definitely worth it though, we now have 700 investors that are all miniature investors and avid fans of ours that are going out there, telling our story and really want us to succeed.

We also put our lives on the line to show that we could succeed, as we wanted to prove to everyone that we could do it. When we moved in with my parents, it was very much, oh we'll be out in six months, but we only moved out two years later!

In lockdown, we ended up going to work making hand sanitiser as well, as we were living with them longer than we thought possible. It was quite a test of our relationships – especially with making the hand sanitiser.

We already had the pieces in to make the hand sanitizer, but we only did it because of the shortage. We gave what we made to key workers at the time, then any excess that we had we sold online and it was just another way to get through the pandemic really.

Home drinking also kept our brewery alive as well, social media definitely came into play because everyone was at home. We had the opportunity to tell our story, to do live posts, and grow.

Everyone ended up loving the hand sanitiser as well, it doesn't hurt your hands and there was actually a local construction company that ended up buying loads from us as they couldn't get it elsewhere.

When you have a business though, with your lives on the line in some ways, you just adjust the best you can and luckily we were there to fill that need.

CHAPTER EIGHTEEN:

BUNMI SCOTT - IT'S ALL ABOUT YOU ECO

WEBSITE: itsallaboutyou.co.uk

It's All About You is an eco-friendly website that aims to help people be more eco-conscious and as shop as plastic free as possible. It also sells private health tests, health food boxes and even vitamin and mineral packs to help people have the freedom to find out what their body really needs and improve their well-being.

As a mum with two kids, it was always so important to make something affordable. I think there's things that everyone can do for the environment but sometimes you have no idea where to start or the options are so costly to make that change.

Originally it was something quite different, we wanted to help people look at their health and really optimise it, and really understand what they're putting in their body. One of the things that I've learned over time though is it's not just about what you put in your body, it's also if you're exercising and the things you're using day-to-day.

Eventually, we decided to try a few eco-friendly projects just to see what happened and people really, really wanted what we offered. So, from there we've grown into a business that's really eco-friendly and sustainable.

We offer a range of food and non-food, and all of our foods have free refills. So you buy as little or as much as you want, and we refill them. We also do refills on a few other things like cleaning products, shampoos, conditioners, etc.

We also resell a range of zero waste products that are our own label, and we have some other brands on board with us as well.

We've always been an online business and we bought the premises with the intention of continuing to stay online. At the time we realised that we also had enough space for a physical store as well, so we incorporated a physical store into the business. It wasn't something we initially had in the plans, but it's one of those things that you see an idea and you think well, we can make it work!

From an online point of view, we've always sold zero waste products online. In terms of sustainability, when lockdown happened we just needed everything to go online. We weren't really sure what was going to happen, or how long we were going to be in lockdown for, so we just put everything online and looked at how we could still do the refills.

In the end, I spent three or four nights putting everything we had available online, then we shut the doors and people could choose to buy as much or as little as they wanted. After that we would pack it all up in paper bags or eco-friendly containers. People then came from all over the country, sometimes in Europe looking for things we could provide for them.

One example is that we never ran out of things like flour or yeast, and everyone wanted them. Everyone was baking bread, cakes or buns - in the first lockdown everyone wanted to bake! So we had a really good constant stream of service and we just adapted to how we sold things to people.

Then our supply chain broke, because of COVID and I laid in bed thinking that there had to be an easier way to get these products. So, we ended up contacting schools, pubs, bars and asking about their products and what their supply chain was, eventually we found a supplier to keep going.

We weren't afraid to look at other options. In the end, we spoke with catering industries that didn't have any business when restaurants were closed and they helped us. I had one supplier in particular that came from further away that had been furloughed and they were so grateful that they could keep working. One man, who was one of our suppliers, told us that our business had helped him keep his job.

As a salesperson, I always had numbers to hit, but it was great knowing that we had a much bigger impact than that. I just couldn't give up, I knew that if I did I'd kick myself for not trying harder.

With supermarkets as well, they have the disadvantage of having to go through a distribution chain. They can't think oh well, we'll just go to a different wholesaler. For us, we had the ability to be flexible and make it work.

On the environmental side of our business, I've always been very passionate about cutting out plastic and waste. Having that passion came through in my social media, I gave tips and educated people to make more informed choices. I think it was really important to make the information accessible, as a lot of people just feel like they're being hammered by businesses who are saying don't do this! Don't do that! Whereas my approach was more, do what you can and make it fit into your lifestyle.

I'm a mum with two kids, not everything works. At one time I tried having glass bottles in my house everywhere but it just was impossible! I'd rather have an eco-friendly plastic bottle that I know I can resell. I've learnt the difference between plastic and what's alright to use. The most important thing to take away from our brand was that people needed to know that the best thing you can do is just to reduce your single waste.

Single use plastic is something that we're trying to get rid of and we're trying to promote things that you can use over and over again. An example is if you use an amazing plastic bottle at home, it works and you keep using it until it doesn't. We want to reduce waste as much as possible and just making those small changes is better than nothing.

We had an initial investment when we set this up to help us with our website. You find these smaller websites that get up and running just fall apart and they're just not working. I wanted to do something that could get a lot of traffic, and investment to get us to a place that had a suitable enough website that people could really use.

Obviously, everything costs a lot of money in business and you find there's a lot of trial and error. Especially when you are doing things that other people haven't done before. You're trying different things to see what fits and trying to move quickly before other people try and do what you're doing.

Nowadays there's a lot of people in the eco stream so I'm getting people contacting me saying that they're opening a little shop, or opening websites, or selling eco products. So there's loads of people that are really into it – and that's why I did this. We have our own branded products, but putting other things on there is great as well.

COVID did restrict things when the lockdowns started happening, but we're just doing what we can. What I noticed in particular was that on our consumer based site, we were doing a lot of bulk orders and we started offering reductions on what people were ordering.

Eventually, in July time I built a wholesale website over a couple of weeks with some products, for people to just go through a wholesale stream. So now, it's just something extra we do in addition to everything else.

With the wholesale, we've also got a link on our customer consumer site – which says "if you are interested in wholesale please click here" they then fill out a form, we look at them, then they are added onto the wholesale site.

As things reopen we're planning on focusing again on sustainability and helping people understand how to be sustainable. I think educating people is really important. Also offering refillable elements to cleaning products, and we're just hoping to continue to find new ways to be sustainable.

Trusting my instincts has been really important throughout the whole business journey as well. Streamlining our business really helped, and removing what didn't work. COVID actually did help us grow a lot, as people had more time online and to try things they wouldn't have otherwise.

Before the lockdowns happened, people were so busy, they had this cycle of leaving early in the morning, working, coming back home, and putting the kids to bed. That cycle is just so busy that you don't really have time to look at what you're doing, especially things like single use plastics – people just use things for convenience.

Before lockdown happened I was just as guilty – there were still things I was using that were single-use, but I started a local refill room to help cut down. There's just so many better ways of doing things and in the first lockdown our waste managed to decrease tremendously.

I think people are also scared of going to refill shops in some ways as well, as they don't really know what to do. But the staff is so friendly and helpful and it's fun for kids. People are scared of new things though and I think if we can show people that something new isn't scary, more people will adjust to that way of living.

CHAPTER NINETEEN:
BIANCA RANGECROFT - WHERING

WEBSITE: whering.co.uk

Whering is a digital wardrobe and personal styling app, it allows you to see everything that you own in one place by taking pictures of what you own. It gives you daily suggestions and curated sustainable product recommendations to complement your clothes.

In June 2020 I was in the headspace where I was trying to be a more eco-conscious customer with where I shopped and how I interacted with what I already owned.

There were no products in the market at the time to really help me style outfits and I really wished there was something like that which existed. In the movie Clueless, one of the characters Cher, has this machine that styles her wardrobes and it just seemed insane to me that in 2020 there was still nothing like that.

It all came from a desire to change that and it was really evident to me that there was nothing in terms of styling outfits. I'd worked on the Stitch Fix IPO when I was with Goldman Sachs in their customer division with retail stocks and I just really wanted to change the way we interacted with clothes as a whole.

There's such a huge throwaway culture with clothes as well, in the UK alone 300,000 tonnes of used clothing goes to a landfill and 5% of the UK's total annual carbon and water footprint comes from clothing consumption.

All these different things eventually led to me creating Whering. It works for you to create your own outfits and styles and is really innovative actually.

You have collections for your summer holidays, packing lists, you have a mood board, a wishlist, etc. It kind of is a one-stop-shop for all your fashion needs and inspiration sets, where your outfits live and we style you but you also get where to buy things sustainably that really fits what you already own.

We spent time building the app over the summer of 2020, then finished it towards the end of September. Finally, we officially launched Whering in February 2021.

We aimed to move really, really fast as we just wanted to get it in the market as soon as possible, it was a bit like a whirlwind in some ways. We managed to get 15,000 users onboarded since our launch as well, so it definitely hit a certain market.

Our main objective was just to make sure that we were building something that women really wanted, to build around a process that was quite complicated really. We did bootstrap everything because we wanted to make sure that we were creating a closed, private and tight-knit community from the get go.

We then transformed the lovely women we had into brand ambassadors and in our community. From there, we looked at things from a product standpoint and marketing one. We made the most of their knowledge, their insights, had focus groups, and from there turned it into a fully-fledged product.

On the tech side, a UX designer said to me when we started that if you don't look back at what you did in the beginning and think it was absolute crap, then you're not moving fast enough or doing well.

We definitely ticked that box! We started off with the concept on Instagram, using your grid, with your clothes, using the stories to style with our clients, then we built the minimum viable product (MVP) and added the basic functions into it. From there, we were able to figure out the machine learning very quickly and extract tags from images.

For example, if you uploaded a white shirt. What does it go with? Then the machine would say, this is how you can style it, what is your style persona? Have you taken our style quiz? Then altogether that adds up and creates a persona for you.

It's a bit like Tinder for clothes really, you swipe yes or no on the outfits we create for you and that validates the learning algorithm we have and helps it pick clothes that are better for you.

When we launched it we were very much in the early stages and had our honeymoon phase. We loved the brand and the initial reception we had of it was really quite positive – especially as it was a product that we've been wanting for the last 15 or so years. Nobody had ever built something like this, so what kept us going when we first launched it was just the positivity around it all from the people who were involved.

The sustainability mission was kind of core to everything that we did as well, and wanted to set up. It made it really easy to identify with like-minded people and get people to share what they were doing.

We ended up having people writing Medium posts about us, doing YouTube videos, leaving us reviews, and it was just all organic. We hadn't asked for any of it in the early stage, so we just had a discussion of what people wanted from us and opened that dialogue.

The key thing though was that we could establish a small community with it all.

We also had a long term and short term plan. The short-term plan was just trying to stay true to letting people have their personal style with the access to a tool like this. Women should be able to style their clothes to their preferences regardless of income levels, privilege, etc and that was really important to us.

Now we've just launched a premium model where you can have added benefits, but the styling functionality is very much like Clueless, and it stays free. You can use your own outfits and style things.

Then in the long-term we're looking at what more women do in the app and trying to tailor it more to them. We're hoping that everything has a purpose and that the supply chain that they're using when they purchase things is more transparent, which will be more sustainable.

When I started out I was also warned that I have to do a lot of networking and really prepare. I watched a talk with Charlene Reed (who is my idol!) on how she raised her first million. She was saying that you basically need to prepare your team for when you're not in the office.

For us, I didn't really get it at first, like we were a tiny team that just went into the market and was wondering how we could fundraise. But then I realised, she was spot on. You really need to have your head in the game even when you're out of the office.

You need to be able to drive a firm with your investors, follow up with a timely manner and it is overwhelming running a company at the same time. It was initially very difficult and on top of that, as cliché as it sounds, it was very hard being a female founder selling this in the fashion field, as the fashion world is already very saturated.

A lot of white, male and middle-aged investors just didn't really under-stand the concept of it. They didn't know why it was such a game changer so we had to really drive our story, paint a picture of where our product was going, why the product matters and how we're capitalising on current trends. We got our first funds from friends and family, but now we're hoping to raise far more later this year.

I think the most important thing is believing you can do it and just not saying no or letting your guard down. When you're a founder of a start-up you need to have the ambition and the drive but also knowing where you've failed, when you need to move on and what you can learn from things.

We're very conscious about pivoting and finding people to help fill gaps in our knowledge. A real key thing is that you can't do everything yourself – nobody can as it's simply impossible. You need to get people in there that are better than you at doing things and admitting that there are people better than you.

Overall though, community has been the most important thing. We're driving this circular model of swapping and sharing things, or even allowing your friends to buy stuff from you which takes out a component of fast fashion. So that's the next step for us, but we're always looking to improve.

Printed in Great Britain
by Amazon

78090925R00068